Leaders in Adversity: The American University of Beirut

Silvia Farouk Fadel, M.Ed

Acknowledgments

To my father, who didn't give me a choice as to where I would pursue my higher education; he was convinced the only place for me would be through the gates of The American University of Beirut. He always told me that my education will always be my weapon in life. He was right.

To my daughters, Asma Eljibahi and Lamees Eljibahi, who I always live to tell stories to. May you always feel empowered to do more than you ever think you will. You are the light of my life.

To my husband, my savior, Haj Lamont. There was a time that this book was left untouched, but you helped me bring it to life.

To my mother: thank you for showing me the characteristics of what a true woman, wife, sister, mother, and friend consists of. I too shall follow your path.

To my siblings: Ahmed, Aboudi, Suraya, Silvana, Rima, Amira, and Ali. Thank you for being there with me in the journey of life and thank you for showing me what true friendship is.

To Samar Mikati: Thank you for allowing me to spend a lot of time at the AUB Jafet Library to undergo my research. Your help and assistance will never be forgotten.

To AUB: bless you. You live in my heart and soul always. Without you, I wouldn't be where I am today.

Preface

This book briefly describes the 1975-1990 Civil War in Lebanon and how the leaders of the American University of Beirut coped with assassinations, kidnappings and student demonstrations on campus during these years of turmoil in Lebanon. Throughout this war, many Lebanese chose to seek refuge by moving to other countries, while others who were considered less fortunate remained in this war-torn country. Some, however, who decided to stay in Lebanon, did not let the war stop them from pursuing an education even if it was in the middle of a war zone. This book will document the leaders whose dedication, leadership skills, vision, and persistence kept the gates of The American University of Beirut open and served as a beacon of light and hope for young men and women who would later share the responsibility of creating a different world from the one handed to them.

I. Introduction & Brief Background of Lebanon and AUB

It is the image of bloodshed and chaos which reminds one of the days of the civil war in Beirut, Lebanon. Growing up in Lebanon and watching Lebanon being ripped apart by warlords and armed citizens was both bewildering and frightening, mainly because the reasons were never clearly understood. When we asked our parents about it, we never received appropriate answers, or maybe we were just too naïve to understand. The images that lived in my memory are cratered buildings due to gunfire and bombings; people crying about their wounds or the loss of loved ones; cars smoldered in the streets along with human corpses, which were too many to count. During this chaotic period, movies were released about hijackers and hostages, which were contemporary themes during that time. My parents were glued to the television watching the country they once knew being destroyed and taken away from them. Even now, Lebanon does not rest; my parents still watch and update themselves with Lebanese news, as they sit in their living room in Los Angeles.

I still get images when we traveled to Lebanon during the summer holidays in the 1980s. It was a dangerous time then, and I could not understand why my parents risked our lives to take us there. I still hear the sounds of gunshot and rockets flying above our summer home. I recall when I also received a gunshot wound to my left leg by a drive-by shooter, who chose to shoot at a group of innocent children walking to a grocery store to buy ice cream in the sweltering summer heat. I also remember memories of family members agonizing over the death of our relatives.

There was one experience that also never left me, and it was during one of the summer visits we made to Lebanon. My grandfather had a home in a village located in the South of Lebanon called Kfartebneit. This beautiful family home was surrounded by a large piece of land where my grandparents grew all kinds of fruits and vegetables. My grandfather's house was situated immediately underneath an Israeli (IDF) occupation located at the highest hilltop area so that the Israeli's would be able to monitor their surroundings easily and have full control of the village. This was common among almost every town in the South of Lebanon.

My family and I, one summer in 1986, were trapped inside my grandfather's home due to constant shelling on the village from the hilltop area that used to haunt me. My entire family hid at the back of the house to avoid any bombardment taking place at the the front of the house, which was directly facing the Israeli occupied hill. I remember when it grew quiet, and we were finally able to go outdoors. While we were outside, British reporters came by my grandfather's home and wanted to interview us since they noticed we were fluent in the English language. The only thing I remember about that interview was me singing 'We are the World' to their tape recorder.

Every time I visit the home of my grandparents, I was always scared to look straight at the hilltop; I always knew they were watching us, and it haunted me throughout my entire childhood each time I were to visit my grandfather. It wasn't until the year 1999, when I was a college student at AUB, that the Israeli's withdrew their occupation in the South of Lebanon; this was a massive victory for the Lebanese people. That same day, my family and I drove to my grandfather's village flying Lebanese flags outside the window of our Mitsubishi Pajero, celebrating this victory among other people driving to the South.

The one thing I wanted to do when I arrived to my grandfather's home was to go to the IDF hilltop that haunted me, my entire childhood, and this is precisely what I did. My father agreed to drive us to the top so we could take a look around, since the IDF evacuated the entire area, however, we were warned to be careful of landmines. Sadly, many Lebanese villagers and children lost limbs or lost their lives after the IDF left. I still wanted to take the risk to overcome my fear of this hilltop. When we arrived, the base was filled with sandbags and rubble. The entire base was made of concrete with surrounding concrete walls to protect it, along with underground walkways and bomb shelters. There was nothing that surprised me as I walked around to see the place that once haunted me; the only aspect that grabbed my attention was looking over at my grandfather's home from the very top. It seemed so peaceful and minuscule.

Now as an adult, when I visit Lebanon, I understand why my parents risked our lives by taking us there during Lebanon's worst moments; Lebanon was their pride, joy, and heritage. Regardless of what Lebanon was going through, they wanted to be there.

Growing up in California, I never imagined I would be a part of this chaotic world, which I knew as Lebanon. However, in 1995, I enrolled at the American University of Beirut (AUB), located in the Ras Beirut area, on a hilly sun-drenched peninsula, and graduated from AUB in 2001 with a Bachelor's in English and a Teaching Diploma in Teaching English as a Second Language. During this time, after the end of the Civil War, what was left were the bullet-pocket buildings filled with uneasy reminders, sandbags still in place under different buildings, along with eerie silhouettes marked out in the interior of each destroyed building. It was during this post-war period, 1992-1998, that Beirut's restoration was carried out under the leadership of Prime Minister (and construction magnate) Rafiq Hariri. Major areas of Beirut were rebuilt, and the memory of the *Green-Line* was demolished.

Unfortunately, Rafiq Hariri was assassinated in 2005 on Valentine's Day in a car-bomb explosion near Beirut's Corniche which ignited the resurgence of war. According to American journalist Joshua Hammer, a veteran foreign war correspondent for *Newsweek*, "Lebanon's darker identity took hold —with car bombs, political chaos and a 34-day war between Hezbollah and Israel in 2006 that left at least 1,000 dead and billions of dollars in damage. Today Lebanon seems trapped between an economically vibrant, tourist-friendly democracy and Islamic radicalism and Arab-world intrigue". On May 25, 2008, General Michel Suleiman was elected President by Lebanon's Parliament after an eighteen-month constitution which left Lebanon without a president and a possibility of another civil war.

The experience of witnessing Rafiq Hariri's reconstruction of Beirut and studying and residing on the campus of the American University of Beirut served as an encouragement to document the courageous and inspirational leaders who guided AUB from 1975 to 1990, a period of violence and an unprecedented chaotic civil war.

A Lebanese Flashback

Lebanon is a small sectarian state in the Middle East which lies on the east side of the Mediterranean and is no bigger than the state of Connecticut. Lebanon was first under Turkish Ottoman rule for about three hundred years before World War I. After World War I, Turkey had suffered a loss from the war and then Lebanon came under European colonial domination. The Civil War began in 1860 when the Druze inflicted massacres on the Maronites. It ended with a French military intervention on the Maronites' behalf and the creation of a new independent order under European protection. During that time, France and Britain divided the Arab provinces among themselves; Syria and Lebanon went under the rule of the French, while Iraq and Palestine fell under British rule.

The Arab nations wanted to be independent states without the rule of the Europeans. Even Daniel Bliss who was President of the American University of Beirut and a resident of the Middle East at the time, pleaded with the American Government to assist in banishing the European forces and giving independence to the Arab states; Bliss's pleas were ignored.

Despite the defeat of the Maronites, they still managed to grow stronger in Lebanon; they gained ground demographically, territorially, educationally and economically; they secured a clear political superiority as well. The Christians in Lebanon and Syria played a significant role in pioneering the Arab awakening; this was due to their long-standing association with the West, and seats of learning, such as the American University of Beirut, which missionaries and philanthropists, both European and American, established among them. The French stood behind and supported the Maronites, who no longer wanted to be ruled under Islamic law as they experienced before with the Ottoman Empire until Lebanon became an Independent country in 1943. During that time, the Maronites were the majority in Lebanon as they numbered 351,197 or 33.57 percent out of the total population of 1,046,164. The Maronites took the presidency, command of the army and other key posts. The Sunnis, numbering 194,305 or 18.57 percent of the people, at the time of the 1932 census, took the premiership. The least favored were the 166,545 Shiites, at 15.92 percent.

To many outside observers, it might appear that Lebanon's Civil War involved Muslims and Christians fighting against one another in the city they divided into their particular zones. It is true that the Christians occupied the Eastern part of Beirut because the Western region was taken over by the Muslims. However, the reality was that the Palestinians, Syrian, and Israeli's were also involved. The Muslims fought with the Christians; various Lebanese organizations battled the Palestinians and Syrians, and the Israeli's clashed with the Arabs. Other sectarian groups were also involved which included Roman Catholics, Maronites, Greek Orthodox, Greek Catholics, and a smattering of Protestants combined, which accounted for an estimated 40 percent of the Lebanese population in 1975. The Druze which stood apart from the Muslim communities claimed 6 percent of the shared population. The Sunni Muslims constituted 22 percent, and the Shiite community was rapidly rising to 32 percent at the time. These clashes between the different sects and organizations made peace nearly impossible.

What used to be a country where Western tourists wanted to sample a taste of the Middle East without having to endure the chaos of Damascus or Cairo, Lebanon was always known as the Paris of the Middle East. Since the Civil War lasted for approximately 15 years, many changes occurred during that time which permanently changed Lebanon and its attraction to Western travelers. During the war, more and frequently changing alliances were organized which impacted who was on which side of the conflict and fighting. Due to this, Beirut was segregated into a sectarian enclave.

II. The Birth of AUB

In 1862 American missionaries in Lebanon and Syria, which were under the American Board of Commissioners, asked Dr. Daniel Bliss (1823-1916) to discover or create a college of higher education which would include medical training. The missionaries were previously in Lebanon and Syria because they wanted to evangelize the area and build an educational infrastructure. The apostles managed to introduce a printing press in Beirut and also established primary schools with over a thousand pupils. As a result, a civil war broke out between Syria and Mount Lebanon in 1860. The missionaries were losing many of their pupils, especially since their pupils were disinterested in completing their studies in religion; they wanted to seek their higher education elsewhere. These pupils were interested in a more liberal education than the knowledge given to them; this is how and why the missionaries decided to provide the region with a more western style of learning by appointing Dr. Daniel Bliss as the founder of an organization which will become the cultural and educational center for Syrian intellectuals as well as the Arab world.

Dr. Daniel Bliss left his evangelistic work of the mission in Lebanon to continue the foundation of what would become a uniquely American institution in Lebanon, as well as the Middle East. The focus of this soon-to-be university was for it to have an American educational character, independent administration from the mission and its source.

During that same year in 1862, Dr. Daniel Bliss traveled back to the United States to request funds to build this new venture. As a result, while Dr. Bliss was trying to raise money for the new institute, the State of New York gave the name of the Institute on April 24, 1863, which was The Syrian Protestant College. One year later, in August 1864, Dr. Bliss raised $100,000. Due to inflation during the Civil War, it was agreed that Dr. Bliss should raise the first-rate fund in England to launch the beginning of the new college. After collecting funds in England, he traveled back to Beirut in March 1866. He chose to build a university on a deserted stretch of land that consisted of dunes, which also served as Beirut's garbage dump. Finally, the college opened on December 3, 1866, with its first class of 16 students. Bliss was elected unanimously as President of the University.

On December 7, 1871, the Treasurer of the Board of Trustees, William E. Dodge, Sr. laid a cornerstone on the first building ever built. During that ceremony, President Bliss expressed the belief of the college by saying, "This college is for all conditions and classes of men without regard to color, nationality, race or religion. A man, white, black, or yellow, Christian, Jew, Mohammedan or heathen, may enter and enjoy all the advantages of this institution for three, four or eight years; and go out believing in one God, in many gods, or no god. But, it will be impossible for anyone to continue with us long without knowing what we believe to be the truth and our reasons for that belief". However, the University was not open for women at the time.

The School of Medicine was established in 1867. After that in 1871, the School of Pharmacy and a preparatory school were included and became independent in 1960. The School came to be known as International College. The School of Commerce which became the Faculty of Arts and Sciences was integrated in 1900. The American University Hospital (AUH) opened in 1905, and as a result of that, a school of nursing was built. Five years later, a school of dentistry was also established.

Under Bliss's control, a diverse curriculum was introduced to the students. The curriculum consisted of languages, sciences, religion, history, geography, philosophy, mathematics, grammar, rhetoric, and of course medical studies. Moreover, the universities name was changed to the American University of Beirut by the Board of Regents of the State University of New York on November 18, 1920. In 1924, AUB admitted its first female student who arrived from Egypt; she was veiled and accompanied by her husband who registered as a special student. Finally, in the early 1950s, many new programs were added. They included The Faculty of Engineering and Architecture, The Faculty of Agricultural and Food Sciences, and The Faculty of Health Sciences. AUB trained much of the political leadership of the Middle East. At least nineteen of those who signed the United Nations charter in 1945 were AUB graduates; therefore, AUB proved to be in the best tradition of what the West had to offer the

Arabs.

III. Lebanon at War: 1975 - 1976

On the morning of April 13, 1975, the Paris of the East

exploded. Gunmen, who were unidentified, were speeding in a car

in Ain El Rummaneh in East Beirut and fired on a church. Four

people were killed, and among them were two Maronite

Phalangists or *"Kataeb"* an organization led by Bachir Jemayel.

Later, on the same day, a Phalangist group killed 27 Palestinians

that were also traveling on a bus in the same area to seek revenge

as the Palestinians were going to their camp called Tal El Zaatar.

This fighting lasted for almost two years, and many military

training camps were established around Lebanon which involved

various movements, leaders, women, children, and kinfolks. As a

result, there was a total of about 29 militia groups that were well-known around the country. The fighting started due to the Muslims demanding political and economic developments (due to poverty) and recognition, while the Christians resisted until the government clamped down on the PLO guerrillas. After the first nine months of fighting, 8,000 lives were lost, and the nation had an estimate of 10 million dollars in losses. Severe destruction resulted in many areas of Beirut and road-blocks by Christians and Muslims became an awful trend in 1975. In these operations, either Muslim or Christian groups stopped cars and demanded identification cards which revealed the religion of each Lebanese citizen. If the citizen was of a different faith, they were either slaughtered or abducted. The U.S. Embassy, located on the coast near the Hotel District, was reported under sniper fire. Christian Falangists moved into the bombed-out remains of the 26-story Holiday Inn, while Muslims seized the fire-gutted Phoenicia Hotel 50 yards away. Kidnappings and counter-kidnappings continued in force. As a result, the Syrian government decided to insert their Saiqa (Vanguards of the Popular Liberation War) army into Beirut; this was a step to assist the Lebanese Government in ridding the Palestinians from the country. The streets were dangerous for anyone to undertake littered with dead bodies while other individuals were claimed missing. According to a 1976 issue of *The Economist*, throughout the first phase of the Lebanese civil war 10,000 – 12,000 people were killed, 30,000 – 40,000 injured and 180,000 people were displaced from one part of Lebanon to the other.

Also, Lebanon did not receive financial help from other countries as much as it wanted and needed. The Crown Prince, King Fahd, said in an interview that Saudi Arabia was not willing to financially assist a nation that would not help itself since this assistance would turn into ashes the next day. A new truce was agreed to almost every week since the war started, but the fighting would start all over again. Lebanon also elected a new President,

Elias Sarkis, to replace Suleiman Franjieh on September 23, 1976.

Sarkis was the Governor of the Central Bank and even a lawyer; he

was not a politician. Elias Sarkis was unable to become President

since Franjieh refused to resign. Three weeks after Sarkis's

election, the leader of the Druze community, Kamal Jumblatt's

only sister, Linda Atrash, was murdered in her apartment in East

Beirut. As Linda opened her front door, unidentified men fired at

her with a submachine gun, while her brother and two daughters

were left severely wounded. Many Lebanese groups, organizations,

and even journalists claimed that this murder was likely caused by

foreigners or Lebanese extremists who wanted to spark a civil war

by blocking a truce. Also, following that event, the Syrians

bombarded Beirut with warplanes for the first time during the

fourteen-month war. The Syrian's intention was to target the

Palestinians and Druze or Leftist organization. By then, it was

estimated that 18,000 to 20,000 people had died since the war started. When a ceasefire and "Green-Line," which divided East

Beirut from the West, was implemented after several months of

fighting, the Lebanese people had hoped for peace, but little did

they know or realize that there were many more years of horror

and destruction to come. Following all of this, Selim Hoss was

appointed Prime Minister on December 9, 1976; Hoss was a well-

educated Sunni Muslim and a professor and banker in economics.

The killings were not acts of senseless individuals because

it involved: Christians against Muslims, Syrians diverging with

Palestinians, the rich fighting the poor, Arab countries clashing

with Israel, the superpowers fighting one another, and politicians

fighting other politicians. The Muslims wanted more power in the

government; the Christians wanted the Palestinians out of

Lebanon; the Syrians wanted the Palestinians to stop meddling in

Lebanon's issues; the Palestinians wished to function freely within

Lebanon politically.

The Israeli's were pleased to see the Syrians (led by Hafez Al Assad) and Palestinians (led by Yasser Arafat) clashing and at the same time took advantage of the Israeli-Lebanese border by trading food across the border. The Americans were aiding Syria and Israel, but did not intend to involve itself within Lebanon's politics as it left its Embassy with only a caretaking staff. All of this was being played out while Lebanon, the country, was not being governed. To make matters worse, by 1976 there was an estimate of three weapons per each Lebanese male citizen.

IV. AUB and President Samuel Kirkwood, 1975-1976

The American University of Beirut began to fall because of its location. AUB, in Ras Beirut, is in the western part of Beirut and opened its doors to educate students from all over Lebanon and the world. The students of AUB are also known to be politically active. According to Boston University Professor and

Author, Betty S. Anderson, "The very first student protest by Arabs took place on this campus – in the 1882 'Darwin' Controversy – and every current of Arab nationalism, Lebanese nationalism, Communism, and Socialism found organized voice there during the course of the 1930s, 1940s, and 1950s". Being at AUB meant that one would try various lifestyles, challenge unexamined belief systems, and benefit from association with men and women who demonstrated the values of a liberal education.

AUB began to face a budget crisis due to the war. The University started to raise tuition fees by 30% and canceled salary increments for teachers and senior staff. Since the war began, it was difficult for classes to meet. The University is just blocks away from the Green Line and the battle zone of the hotels. Some stray shells landed on campus. However, the University did not experience critical hostilities; roadblocks also prevented students, faculty, and staff from traveling to school which led to many absences. In a 1975 memorandum, the Dean of the Faculty of Engineering and Architecture, Raymond S. Ghosn, wrote there were several days in which faculty members, staff, and students could not leave their homes or were unable to reach campus because of the clashes.

Dr. Samuel B. Kirkwood was President of the American University of Beirut between the years of 1965 – 1976. He came to AUB as Dean of the Faculty of Medical Sciences in 1962 and was commissioner of the Department of Health in Massachusetts from 1953 until 1958 and was later Senior Administrator of the United States Agency for International Development in Iran. Dr. Kirkwood was AUB's seventh president and worked hard to keep AUB operating during adverse times such as the Arab-Israeli wars, strikes, demonstrations, upheavals, and the civil war in Lebanon. During the time of the budget crisis, Dr. Kirkwood claimed that 6.5 million dollars was needed to meet the University's expenses and if the University was unable to receive such financial assistance, their

doors would be closed in April 1976. In a 1975 interview, Dr.

Kirkwood stated, "The University is in the midst of the city, which

is a victim of factional fighting of the worst order. The problems

we face if we do not get tuition money coming in are

insurmountable, while we are committed to keeping the university

going as long as possible, we had to make a realistic assessment.

We'll run to the last dollar, and then if we don't get the money we

need, that's it". According to a correspondent from *The Economist,*

the reason AUB did not receive much financial assistance from

neither the American nor Arab nations was that The United States

Government thought that AUB students were too pro-Arab and

anti-American, while the Arab nations found AUB students too

pro-American and anti-Arab. Dr. Kirkwood, however, seemed

positive about receiving support from the American and Lebanese

government by saying, "Plans are based upon a firm belief in the future of the university, that AUB will receive the support necessary to survive the present circumstances."

In contrast to Kirkwood's statement, a senior faculty member claimed that their lives were at risk due to their career at AUB and that the future did not seem to be very positive. As a result, by January 2, 1976, the Lebanese government decided to approve AUB a loan to assist its financial burden. As a result of the decision, the Minister of Education, Ghassan Tueni, explained to the Cabinet the consequences that Lebanon would face if the University were to close down.

Some saw Dr. Kirkwood as a leader who did not truly inspire others around him. He had his entourage of colleagues, which he surrounded himself with and they were defenders of the American policy in the Middle East; this led students to lose most of their rights or freedom with the suspicion of being spied on by the campus security guards. Therefore, this led the students to either be suspended or dismissed due to their student unions or groups. Others, however, felt genuinely inspired by Kirkwood's leadership. At one of the student strikes on campus during the early 1970s, Kirkwood left his office in College Hall and went to the West Hall to talk to the demonstrating students. Amidst a great deal of commotion and shouting, President Kirkwood started to speak. Almost immediately there was calm, as the students strained to hear Kirkwood's softly spoken words.

It is critical for leaders to establish trust among members of their environment for success in any institution. It is the role of the leader, no matter what position they are in, to set the stage for establishing this environment of trust. In terms of a Western leader, leading an institution outside of their home country, this leader must have understanding of those whom they would seek to influence by understanding their core beliefs and values. Since there was no sense of trust among students and the leadership of their University and due to the political strife, the University closed its doors during the fall 1975 semester and the President announced that AUB's doors would open January 5, 1976, for at least two more semesters.

For an American president to lead such a university in the Middle East, this president must have cultural understanding and tolerance for religious beliefs within a particular environment. According to a "declaration of principles" by the American Association of University Professors (AAUP), "Such an institution must be prepared to tolerate a range of views on controversial issues. It must also tolerate those members of its faculty who expressed such aberrant views. Academic institutions that sought to repress or silence such views, simply did not deserve the respect of the higher education community." A leader of an institution of higher education should not take sides when it comes to political or social issues; instead, they should be tolerant and understanding about the views of individuals in their community.

AUB managed to open its doors to 2000 students either living on or off campus during the first week of January 1976. During that time, the Office of the Registrar claimed that enrollment was rising and falling with the rise and fall of fighting. However, on February 17, 1976, an expelled Palestinian student by the name of Najem Najem entered the AUB campus and shot and killed both Professor Robert Najemy, Dean of Students, born in Massachusetts to Lebanese immigrated parents, and Professor Raymond Ghosn, Dean of School of Engineering and Architecture. Najem first shot Professor Najemy by breaking into his office; Professor Ghosn entered the office to find out what had happened and as a result, he was also killed. Najem then broke into the office of George Hakim, the Vice President of AUB, and held him and five other AUB employees' hostage until Najem was detained by police and Palestinian security guards. However, before Najem could be secured, an employee at the University shot Najem; this employee was also arrested.

AUB remained closed between the months of March and May 1976 due to fighting between Christian and Muslim militants. The United States advised all American citizens to leave Lebanon immediately. That year, about 600 Americans were evacuated by sea to Greece including members of the American Embassy and diplomatic staff. However, most of the professors and doctors of AUB and AUB Medical Center remained in the country. Don Meyer, Director of Operations at AUB, wrote in a 1976 interim report: "The continued political and military disturbances are still severely hampering the University. In most areas non-academic attendance is at approximately the 25% level with a number of employees, sleeping in their offices or work areas." The leadership of AUB offered accommodation for its faculty and staff on campus to ensure their safety; this gives an example of how President Kirkwood empathized with members of his community by allowing permanent accommodation for those who found it difficult to commute to or from their homes either before or after their working hours.

During this two-month interruption of the academic program between March 15 – May 14, 1976, the new Military Commander of Beirut declared an immediate curfew because of the military takeover by a modern "Reform Movement." As a result, after ten years of leading AUB, Dr. Samuel Kirkwood announced his resignation on March 22, 1976, which was a dangerous time for the University. Dean Craig Lichtenwalner was then designated as Acting President and had to assist in dealing with three major concerns: the continued operation of the American University Hospital (although it had limited staff), the resumption of the undergraduate studies (which was already delayed for some time), and for the Lebanese government to provide AUB with the 10.5 million dollar loan it promised to meet the payroll needs.

Two days after Dr. Kirkwood resigned from AUB, the University was deeply shaken on March 24, 1976. A Penrose Hall student was killed by shrapnel from a mortar, as he was making a phone call at the reception desk of his dorm. The following day, a second mortar exploded in the Penrose Hall garden at noon just 25 feet from the first mortar. Twelve others were injured including the son of the Vice President of AUB, Dr. George Hakim, who was taken to London for treatment due to a complicated upper leg fracture. During the suspension of classes in March 1976, most of the 1200 students that were living on campus left for home, and the number dropped to 250 students, both male and female dorm students. All social activities were confined in the dormitories; students residing in the dorms volunteered in the nearby American

University Hospital but faced financial difficulty since they were unable to obtain cash from banks due to closure of banks, so the University offered these students meal vouchers; this helped solve the problem of some of the student's needs which offered them a sense of motivation to remain on campus to further their education. The events of the attacks on the men's dormitory also led up to two days of rocket firing from the AUB Green Field located along the coast of Ras Beirut, when armed men broke into the campus from the sea gate. The sons and daughters of faculty members (some American) were playing on the AUB Green Field as the armed men gathered the kids at gunpoint to hold them hostage until a university official faced these armed men and convinced them to let the kids go. Another university official approached the armed men and protested not to fire any weapons from the campus since it would bring probable retaliation devastation to the University and its hard-working students. After the armed men fired six rounds of artillery towards the Christian port area to the North, they packed their weapons and left by nightfall. Fortunately, retaliation towards the University did not occur.

Due to the tension between East and West Beirut, delayed radio and television announcements were made to students and faculty to inform them about the status of the University. In 1976 George Hakim, Vice President of AUB noted, "Special attention was given to making it clear to faculty and students that they should not expose themselves to personal danger in order to attend class. There was also an effort to assure students who are unable to meet their classes that they could make up academic requirements in the second semester and receive full credit."

By May 27, 1976, classes resumed at the University, and a total number of 3,098 casualties had been treated at AUB's American University Hospital since the civil war started in April

1975. AUB owned a large estate of land for agricultural studies and experimentation in the Bekaa mountains, located in the eastern part of Lebanon. However, the farm was being used as a military base for Lt. Ahmad Khatib's Army which constituted 1,500 men. Although the army occupied this vast estate, the AUB staff still managed to operate the produce grown on the farm.

When classes resumed in May, AUB had still not received a greater share of the loan it requested from the Lebanese government; this affected the morale of the faculty members who were risking their lives by leaving their homes to attend work or classes. Approximately half of the expatriate faculty residents in campus housing left the country on an emergency leave; the majority moved to other Middle Eastern countries or Europe. Meetings with chairpersons of departments and programs and with the faculty as a whole (formally and informally) were held to give information on the current crisis and to provide an opportunity for discussion on a wide-ranging basis and on all issues in which the

faculty was concerned.

As the academic year came to a close, Richard Mishalani,

the Acting Director of the Physical Plant Department at the

American University of Beirut, reported in a 1976 Interim Report

that the exchange of shelling between the various sectors of Beirut

resulted in $22,600 of damage to the University.

V. Invasions & Assassinations Outside AUB's Gates, 1977-1982

The next stage of the Civil War between 1977 and 1981

involved the assassination of Kamal Jumblatt on March 16, 1977.

Kamal Jumblatt was the leader of the Druze community and an

author of many political books. He allied himself with the

Palestinians and other Muslim partners, but urged the Syrians to

keep out of Lebanon; however, as he was traveling in his car, he was ambushed in Moukhtara, a mountain road, while he was on his

way home. His son, Waleed Jumblatt who was twenty-seven years

old at the time, then found himself the leader of the Druze

community. This event sparked fear that another civil war would

begin after a cease-fire began in November 1976. As a result, in

April 1977, *The New York Times* reported, "More than 600,000

Lebanese, about 20 percent of the population, fled the country

during the recent civil war… almost half the emigrants – 272,500 –

settled permanently outside Lebanon, including 14,515 in the

United States". Later in July 1977, fighting broke out again in a

Palestinian refugee camp where a pro-Syrian faction and Iraqi-

backed radicals battled with one another leaving many guerillas

wounded. Many people in the area were then urged to stay indoors

due to the threat of constant fighting. However, in the mountain

area of Chuf, Lebanon, the Druze which out-numbered the

Christian Maronites were battling as the Christians, who were getting support from the Israeli's, were also fighting the Palestinians in the south of Lebanon. Even ten months after the Civil War, Beirut was still divided into two cities. West Beirut was an area which was known for its hotels, foreign embassies, government buildings, schools, restaurants, shops, entertainment, and beaches, while East Beirut was more of a residential area that consisted of working-class citizens. East Beirut became a stifling and over-crowded place that was uncomfortable for many residents.

By February 1978, the Syrian peacemaking troops, which brought peace in 1975-1976 in Lebanon, clashed with the Lebanese Army for the first time since the Lebanese Civil War ended. The incident began at a Syrian road-block where a Lebanese army recruit disputed with Syrian military men in East Beirut. Journalist Robert Fisk described this by saying, "Syria had come to Lebanon and Syria was now being corrupted by Lebanon, as surely as another great army would soon be corrupted.

Lebanon's revenge was to welcome all her invaders and then kiss

them to death."

In March 1978, the United Nations forces not only had a

hard time separating the Lebanese-Israeli border by keeping Israel

out of Lebanon since its invasion in March, but also, had a hard

time dealing with the heavily armed Christian militia in that area.

The UN estimated a six-month budget of 68 million dollars for its

foreign army which consisted of 6,000 men from France, Ireland,

Norway, Senegal, Nigeria, Holland, Finland, Fiji, Nepal, Ghana,

and the Shah's Iranian army.

The killings of President Sleiman Franjieh's son Tony

Franjieh who was 36-years-old, his wife, and two-year-old

daughter by the Phalangist militia was another major incident.

Tony Franjieh and his wife witnessed the shooting of their

daughter, and then Tony witnessed the killing of his wife before he was killed. The murders were a result of the former president

opposing the Maronite alliance for siding with Israel. This

gruesome killing had the President of Lebanon call for the

obliteration of all Phalangists in Lebanon which seemed to be

happening as Franjieh's supporters also fled to West Beirut (which

was a Muslim area) to escape threats of Phalangists. Fisk recalled,

"These were strange times for the Lebanese, months in which

political patterns merged and then parted as if in a kaleidoscope,

the symmetry of each new hostility, of threat and settlement, fused

into a new dimension."

Syrian troops turned against its allies and caused massacres

in the Christian area over the Green Line, and Mount Lebanon as

well. Due to this, Israel sent jets flying over Beirut to deliver a

sonic boom which was a threat to Syria to stop the killings of the

Christians. Soon after, Israel added to the great destruction of

Lebanon by bombarding the central district of Beirut as well as the southern cities such as Saida and Nabatieh. Israel sent in 25,000 troops from three axes of the country. It was the first to ever hit a residential area, especially in Beirut by launching bloody attacks against Lebanon. Israel invaded Lebanon by bombarding it by the air, sea, and land. According to Robert Fisk, the Israeli's consistently described the Palestinians as 'terrorists.' However, he added, "If the word was to be used, it should apply to the terrorists on Israel's side."

American citizens were advised to leave as all dependents of the U.S. embassy personnel evacuated Lebanon in July 1978. U.S President Carter urged that the UN Security Council approve the Resolution 436 for a ceasefire in Lebanon; however, clashes between the Israeli forces and the Palestinians commenced by January 1979. During 1980 a stage of death threats, bombing incidents, kidnappings and murder developed against journalists, both Western and local. Scores of artillery and weapons were also pouring into Lebanon. Damascus sent their ammunition by road to Southern Lebanon to supply the Shia Amal movement. Libya supplied Walid Jumblatt's Druze army across the borders of Syria and the Chouf mountains. Israel provided weapons to the Phalange army by boat in the Jounieh port area, while the Palestinians were given their share of the supply from Warsaw. By 1981 Israel broke an accord or agreement to not attack the Syrian army on Lebanon's grounds by firing at a Syrian helicopter on April 28, 1981. Soon, Lebanon began to be a battlefield for other countries.

VI. AUB President Harold Hoelscher, 1977-1981

A graduate in Chemical Engineering from Princeton University and an MA and Ph.D. in Chemical Engineering and Mathematics in Washington University, Dr. Harold Hoelscher served as Dean of the School of Engineering at the University of

Pittsburgh. He also was a member of the Board of Trustees of the American University of Cairo. The AUB Board of Trustees named Dr. Harold Hoelscher President of AUB effective July 1, 1977, where he remained until 1981.

After nineteen months of the Civil War, registration at AUB finally increased to about 3,000 students and continued to rise as Dr. Harold Hoelscher was appointed President of the University. According to the Office of the Registrar, the University consisted of 37% Sunni Muslims, 19.2% Greek Orthodox, 8.6% Maronites, 7.5% Shiite Muslims, 6.7% Druze, and 2.3% Roman Catholics. Another positive and significant stage after the appointment of Dr. Hoelscher was that AUB held its first graduation ceremony in four years since the Civil War started.

Dr. Harold Hoelscher approached the future with optimism and was on a constant move by visiting Lebanese government officials, meeting with University officials, faculty members, alumni and business leaders in the country, and also visited many countries in the Middle East such as Kuwait, Bahrain, The United Arab Emirates, and Qatar. The purpose of his visits was to make acquaintances with key individuals in the region to inform them about AUB's progress and continued operation. He also provided these key individuals information about the available and qualified faculty members, the students, and the programs AUB had at the time. According to Dr. Hoelscher in his 1977 interim report, "I have made it clear in all such visits that I was not, at this time, coming to request financial assistance but, simply, to learn. I indicated that I plan return visits to discuss possible financial assistance when our planning is complete in the near future."

Communication, here, is a significant factor when it comes to leadership. It is vital that leaders communicate and network with those around them for better future relationships and assistance.

The core of effective leadership is delivering 98 percent of a leader's time. At a time, like the Lebanese Civil War, it is necessary for a leader of an institution of higher education to educate other leaders about their university rather than stay within the boundaries of their office. Old relationships need to be maintained, and new ones need to be established, as individuals in crucial positions change, the organizations changes, and the external environment changes. As a result of Dr. Hoelscher's visits to key leaders, His Highness Sheikh Zayed Bin Sultan Al-Nahyan, former ruler of the United Arab Emirates (ruler of the state of Abu Dhabi at the time), generously made a contribution of one million dollars for the Arts and Sciences Department, which then was named Sheikh Zayed Chair of Islamic Studies. Even though the University received such funds, President Hoelscher was still keen on fundraising and holding a primary capital campaign. In his 1977 letter to Dr. Calvin Plimpton, the Chairman of the Board of

Trustees, he wrote: "The University if currently operating on a rock bottom, bare bones budget…as you well know. However, the stark realities of this have become apparent to me only in the last three weeks. Money is not available on this budget for maintenance, for still further changes in faculty salaries, for student activities, for publications, for research and for a host of other things necessary to qualify education. I think we can continue with this bare bones balance budget for about two years. At that time there must be evidence for us that a substantial change in the character of the University finances is possible. In a period of that order we must see a one- to two-hundred million dollar endowment light at the end of a not-too-long tunnel."

Throughout both Fall 1977 and Spring 1978 semesters, the AUB campus remained in session and peace. Students halted protesting on campus by becoming politically inactive, and political posters were no longer seen during that time on the walls of the University. In 1978, President Hoelscher noted, "The flare-

up of fighting in the Eastern sector of the city was considered a

serious threat for a time but seems to have been brought under

effective control by cooperation among all Lebanese groups, the

Government of Lebanon and the representatives of the

Government of Syria." The on-campus activities that took place

during that time involved social activities, and the University's

President was always optimistic about AUB's and Lebanon's

future. Dr. Hoelscher was inaugurated as AUB's eighth president in

a formal AUB inauguration ceremony on February 24, 1978. At the

inauguration, Dr. Hoelscher spoke about re-examining the mission

of the AUB based on the societal changes that surround the

University. By making such changes, AUB needed to seek a unique

educational environment by ensuring excellence and a learning

environment to prepare the students to become effective leaders of

the Middle East in the future. "That future involves dimensions requiring bold concepts and innovative approaches. We must not be isolated from our environment. We must be deeply involved in the reconstruction of The Lebanon and actively engaged in the development of this region," Hoelscher said in his 1978 inauguration speech. During a difficult time in Lebanon, Dr. Hoelscher also stressed that AUB would be an atmosphere of freedom of speech and opinions as well as respect for human dignity, and respect for different minds or opinions; the result of this would lead students to learn to have an understanding for one another and this would direct them to become better leaders in the future. In support of this, Dr. Elie Salem, from the Faculty of Arts and Sciences said, "Human dignity and human difference with dignity are the necessary starting points. All response must find its roots in reason."

Following the inauguration, Mr. Samir Thabet was appointed Vice President, and Mr. David Dodge was named Vice

President for Administration of AUB in March 1978. Dr. Hoelscher ensured that the Board of Deans met weekly to discuss activities, problems, and revision of policies.

Chairing meetings is a critical skill which an academic leader possesses and most of the powers of chairing are immediately useful. It is vital that a leader of higher education forms a sense of direction by putting these directions forward in a meeting. AUB became active in holding many special events on campus regardless of the conflicts that occurred outside its gates. In 1978, Hoelscher stated, "Finally, AUB has become again an active center for cultural and social activities for the city. There were 32 musical concerts, seven performances of two plays, 23 public lectures, 44 film shows, plus play readings, exhibitions of books, art, photography, fashions, industrial products, and a variety of sport and game tournaments."

Campus security was not a significant concern at the time although there were some unpleasant circumstances such as politically oriented posters hung on campus, which was a discouraging practice by the students at the University. There was also concern about what happened outside the walls of the University, which made it difficult for members of the University to move around freely. In a closing note of the President's interim report on the status of AUB's operation, he said, "While much has been accomplished during this past year, there remains much to be done. However, the faculty, staff, and administration of AUB approach the future with feelings of cautious optimism and full determination."

As a result of the positive outlook brought by the new leadership on campus, the Vice President of the University wrote a status report on the 300 days in perspective of AUB. At the time, he witnessed remarkable changes at the University (as the new leadership assumed its role on campus) by how the morale of the faculty has become very high in comparison to how it was. He also mentioned that before the new leadership, there were rumors that AUB would close or be relocated to other countries, but the University prevailed. In 1978, the Vice President said, "Vapors of lead and mercury floated over the Campus…It is against this background that the remarkable changes occurred with students, faculty and staff. The students have, on the whole, performed with maturity in spite of difficult circumstances and, in some instances, with responsibility; the faculty has regained confidence and is eagerly planning for the future; the staff if rallying and, in spite of tempting offers from outside, is betting on AUB. During that year the total number of students registered at the University reached 3721 students who was a 69 percent increase of registered students."

When the summer of 1978 approached, the crisis in

Lebanon intensified. It became severe and potentially dangerous to

AUB. In August 1978 a teenage son of a professor at AUB went

missing after he was last seen in his car outside of his parent's

home in Beirut. AUB personnel made substantial efforts to locate

him and the vehicle he was in; AUB personnel involved both the

Lebanese and Syrian governments, the United States Embassy and

other political groups in Lebanon to assist with this search. His

whereabouts remained unknown.

Shelling increased at the beginning of the month of

October; however, AUB commenced its Fall semester in a timely

manner on October 5, 1978. "Throughout the many difficulties of

the past four months, the AUB Campus remained calm, and an

atmosphere of 'business as usual' prevailed," Hoelscher exclaimed.

Dr. Hoelscher began to continue with fundraising efforts for the

University. He had already spent three weeks in Europe and the

United States during the month of September 1978, and devoted

much of the same efforts in the months of October and November

with the management team of the Vice President and Vice

President for Administration in charge of the University while Dr.

Hoelscher was away. According to Hoelscher, "The management

'Team' of AUB is proving to be a close-knit, cogent and

cooperative groups." AUB was already starting its 113th year of

operations at the time. During the fall semester as students and

faculty were returning to AUB, there became a problem with

housing the faculty, staff, and students on campus. Many members

of staff and faculty, and students found difficulty in commuting

from AUB to their homes, so the majority wanted to be housed on

campus for security and workforce measures. The University was

losing manpower since many members of the faculty would not

show up to work because of commuting difficulties as a result of

the conflicts on the streets. Therefore, staff members were housed in empty spaces in campus buildings, dormitories, and faculty

apartments. Faculty apartment rents also increased by 25%. Since

the female dorms were unable to accommodate all the female

students, and there was free space in the New Men's Dorms

(currently called Kerr Hall), the females were temporarily assigned

to use the first two and a half floors of the men's dormitory along

with segregation and security measures.

AUB held an opening ceremony as it opened its doors in

the Fall 1978 semester and Dr. Hoelscher was there to give a

convocation address. He welcomed and introduced the new leaders

of the university, faculty, and students by offering words of

inspiration to them. Hoelscher also spoke about the mission of

AUB by saying, "We must ask where we can uniquely make our

contribution. What is our academic role? Our mission? How may

we realize our objectives? Through what programs and program

structures? Our mission is to prepare those who will lead the region from chaos into a new future different in both degree and kind from the past. We start a new year with hope, with conviction, and with many difficult tasks before us. I ask the fullest cooperation of all our students, our faculty, our alumni and our many friends to meet these tasks together and overcome each in turn."

When a person is made a leader, they are not necessarily given a crown, but they are given the responsibility of bringing out the best in others. For this reason, leaders need to be trusted, and they will be trusted as long as they demonstrate candor, giving credit to others, and staying real. Although the President was keen on bringing out the best of the AUB graduates to become future leaders, there was already a list of AUB alumni who played a role throughout the region according to a partial listing of alumni. There were already 31 alumni serving as ministers of government or positions of equivalent rank, 9 ambassadors of their government to the United Nations or other countries, 31 director generals (or in equivalent public sectors positions), 59 chairmen of boards, presidents, directors or in positions of equal rank in private sector companies, 22 education leaders (president, deans, etc..) in the region, and others serving in parliaments, senates and positions of significance within the secretariats and political parties of the area.

During the Spring 1979 semester, operations at AUB was running smoothly. The most alarming development during that time were two incidences of break-ins/attempted robbery on campus and a break-in/attempted robbery and mugging at an AUB faculty home off-campus which were both unsuccessful. These common break-ins were as a result of the increasing frequency of physical violence for money. According to Dr. Hoelscher, the problems that were classifiable at AUB were physical issues such as limitations of space, water, oil, and other sources.

Dr. Hoelscher made trips to in the Arab region such as Syria, Dubai, and Abu Dhabi to recognize alumni that have donated large sums of money to AUB. Alumni in Sharjah, United Arab Emirates also invited Dr. and Mrs. Hoelscher to their Annual Ball and presented a $12,850 check as a contribution towards the AUB Alumni Scholarship and Loan Fund. Dr. Hoelscher also met with the Minister of Foreign Affairs, Khalifah al-Sowaidi in Dubai to discuss his support to the Center for Arab and Middle Eastern Studies as a formal proposal was also presented to His Excellency Sheikh Zayed Al Nahyan, ruler of Abu Dhabi at the time, also further supported this Center. There were encouraging results of gifts received in 1979 in comparison to the year 1978. In 1979, AUB received 357 donations which totaled to the amount of $1,366,014, while in 1978 AUB received 108 gifts which totaled to the amount of $813,733. Through the networking and energy that

Dr. Hoelscher put in visiting key personnel to assist in raising

funds had helped the University survive on incoming gifts.

By March 1980, Dr. Hoelscher claimed that AUB

functioned much like any institution of higher education. The

concern that he had was trying to admit students from other parts

of Lebanon and other parts of the world in the upcoming years. "If

AUB is to be a truly regional institution, it then must find ways of

admitting students from Qatar, from Dubai, from Bahrain, from

Saudi Arabia, from the Sudan, from Bangladesh, along with those

highly qualified students who come to us from IC, from

Brummana, and other secondary schools in Lebanon," Dr.

Hoelscher noted.

The Board of Trustees noted in a November 1980 report

that it was crucial for AUB to raise the student tuition fees if the

University intended to remain financially viable. There was a 15%

increase for the non-medical faculties and a 20% increase for the Medical Faculty effective October 1, 1980. In support of the rise of tuition fees, Dr. Hoelchser wrote in a 1980 memo to Dr. C.H. Plimpton, "Tuition must continue to increase as long as inflation makes it necessary. For private universities income from tuition fees is important for survival, while it is less so for government-supported universities." The students entered the University without questioning the rise in tuition fees. The Board of Trustees also emphasized that they did not want their campus "politicized", instead they apparently wanted the students to be structured in their active involvement on campus related to student needs by setting up a student council on campus.

A significant move which the President of AUB and the Board of Trustees made was meeting with the leaders of the political militias and parties. The AUB leaders met with Mr. Yasser Arafat and Mr. Basel Akl of the Palestinian Liberation

Organization (PLO), Mr. Walid Jumblatt and Mr. Inam Raad of the

PPS, Sheikh Shams Eddine of the Higher Shiá Islamic Council for

Lebanon, and with Mr. Samir Sabbagh of the Sunni Murabitoun.

By having the AUB leaders meet with these political leaders that

were involved in major parts of the Lebanese Civil War, the AUB

leaders approached these individuals during a time of crisis and the

more openly they spoke about a problem, its causes, and its

solutions, the more trust they earned from one another inside the

organization and out.

During a crisis, trust is what you need at every turn. The

AUB leaders that met with political parties and movements also

explained the University policies to them to solicit their help in

keeping the University away from factional politics. In 1980, Dr.

Holescher stated, "I was assured that they would assist. I believe

they will."

Dr. Holescher made another convocation speech at the Opening Ceremony of AUB's start of the 115th academic year. This time, Dr. Hoelscher emphasized the theme of the year to be focused on continuity, change, and progress. "In spite of all our problems both internal and external, I remain optimistic about our future. AUB will continue to serve this region by producing yet another generation of leadership. It will continue to be an Arab World center for scholarships, for inter-cultural pursuits and for professional development. It will continue to be a university fully consonant with its traditions. It must," he said.

In 1981, a Student Council was finally organized with the help of faculty members at AUB. Hoelscher noted, "This University-level committee will give attention to matters of legitimate student concern on both the academic and administrative side of the institution. In my opinion, this new system is a considerable achievement and will serve us well for a number of years". On the other hand, some critical problems began to arise on behalf of AUB's President. Dr. Hoelscher was accused of leading an excessive ratio of Christians to Muslims in all the University's activities. This allegation was made by the President of the Islamic Council, Sheikh Ahmad Assaf, who requested swift action to redress this issue. As a result of this, President Hoelscher asked two members of the University to meet with Sheikh Assaf and assure him that AUB's intention and good faith of being unbiased.

Escalation of the local crisis began to rise at the beginning month of April 1981. Some students and employees were unable to come to the campus as there was and exceeded 25% of absenteeism. Housing was provided for essential employees who found it difficult to commute, and cots were set up in dormitory style in different locations of buildings on campus.

By May 23, 1981, President Harold Hoelscher resigned from AUB in a dispute with political implications. Dr. Hoelscher said in a Beirut newspaper interview that he was sharply criticized by Dr. Calvin Plimpton, Chairman of the Board of Trustees, who demanded that Dr. Hoelscher resign. He also mentioned that Dr. Plimpton claimed that Hoelscher was a dictator who politicized the university by establishing relations with local politicians. The Vice President for Administration, David S. Dodge was given full authority to operate the University as Acting President effective June 1981. The campus once again was becoming to be a target exposed to strayed bullets and students were advised to avoid open spaces. Near the university, the three rockets were also fired at the United States Embassy. Besides all this, AUB continued its classes besides the fact that other university's nearby were entirely or partially suspended.

VII. Outside of AUB Gates, 1982-1984

On June 4, 1982, Israel attacked the Sports Stadium in the capital

of Lebanon, claiming that it was a Palestinian target that stored

ammunition belonging to the Palestinians, and Israel officially

invaded Lebanon on June 6, 1982. Now, Lebanon had the presence

of four armies; the Lebanese, Palestinian, Syrian, and the Israeli

military. Afterward, the Lebanese police took control of the streets

of West Beirut and Prime Minister Shafiq Al-Wazzan said he

wanted to hear no more of East and West and had the Green-Line

erased, which gave both the Muslims and Christians the chance to

cross the lines they had not passed since 1975.

In the summer of 1982, a group of kidnappers managed to

smuggle David Dodge, Acting President of the American

University of Beirut, from the AUB campus to Iran. Robert Fisk

described the scene like the following: "According to a Palestinian

student who witnessed the kidnapping, two gunmen in a Renault estate wagon pulled up next to Dodge as he was walking past the University's West Hall. When the American refused to get into the car, one of the men leapt from the vehicle and hit him on the back of the head with the butt of his pistol". Dodge was seen by a campus security guard lying unconscious at the back seat of the car. David Dodge was released a year later with the help of the Syrians."

At this same time, Bashir Gemayel became the new President of Lebanon, but was later killed on September 14, 1982, in his Beirut headquarters in less than a month of his candidacy. The "strong man of Lebanon" was blown to bits. After Bashir's death, his brother Amin Gemayel was elected President. Unlike his brother who was leading the Phalangists, Amin Gemayel kept a low profile and was not involved with such forces. On September 16, 1982, another major attack took place, and it was the atrocious *Sabra Wo Shatilla* attacks where the Israeli army allowed the

Phalangists to enter the Palestinian camp to root out terrorist cells, but nearly 2,000 were massacred within two days of butchery, including women, children, and the elderly. 1982 was a dreadful year for Lebanon, and by the closing of this year, conflicts were still increasing.

President Amin Gemayel had a lot on his agenda once he became President. One significant achievement since the start of the Civil War, was the Lebanese army finally took control and patrolled the streets of Beirut, which the Israeli's abandoned and remained in the South. The Syrians stayed in the North and the Bekaa area. The Palestinians also evacuated Beirut and settled in Tripoli (North Lebanon), while other PLO forces traveled by ship to the country of Tunisia. In a speech President Gemayel made to the Lebanese troops, he said, "We have the responsibility of saving Lebanon and liberating it. The eyes of the world are on us. You must make all citizens feel you are their army." However, fighting broke out in Tripoli at the start of the new year in 1983, but the

major war was in the mountain area of Shuf; the Druze were

battling the Maronites and the Lebanese Army. The Druze were

shelling the Beirut International Airport and the lower regions of

the cities because they wanted a more significant role in the

government with the support of Syria backing them. Due to the

Druze resistance, the Israeli army moved out of the Druze

controlled areas leaving the Christians and Druze fighting and the

Druze shelling East Beirut from their mountainous area, which

opened the stage for a new civil war.

On August 28, 1983, the Lebanese Army lost full control of

Beirut to the militiamen in a matter of one day; The Shiite Muslims

from the *Amal* militia exchanged blows with the Lebanese army.

The small incident started when the Shiite Muslims were holding a

fifth anniversary of the disappearance of their spiritual leader,

Imam Moussa Sadr, when a car passed by and started shooting at the Shiites. The Lebanese army sent troops over to protect the

Muslims, but the military was under attack by snipers and

militiamen, and the event erupted into another full-scale war. The

battle lasted for three days with hundreds of causalities until the

Lebanese Army, which was trained by U.S. Marines Advisors, re-

took control of West Beirut. However, in the mountains, the Druze

were still at war towards the end of the year against the Maronites

who were encouraged by the Israeli army to move into the areas

controlled by the Druze. The Druze leader, Jumblatt, claimed that

the Druze were at a state of war against the Gemayels where the

President, Amin Gemayel, was commanding the Phalangists as

well as the Lebanese Army and was disliked for being pro-

Christian. The Druze moved around freely in the mountains,

without the presence of Israel. The Druze surrounded many towns

including Dar Al Qamar where many innocent lives were lost. By

the end of the year, the United States was also involved when the

U.S. battleship, *New Jersey*, entered the scene of the war like an American movie and began attacking the Druze in the mountains as well as Syrian positions around Beirut, while threats of hostages of U.S. citizens became a reality as other U.S. Marine forces were holding their grounds at the Beirut International Airport by struggling to keep it open so that normal life would return once again. France also sent its troops into Lebanon as protagonists to retaliate against anti-government forces. It was a bad year for the Christians; they lost control of an area over-looking Beirut in the mountain area, while the Muslim-led militia also took control over West Beirut from the Christian-led army, including the loss of lives.

There were more memorable events in 1984. In the United States, Ronald Regan was elected President of the U.S. for a second term. By then, the Civil War in Lebanon had already claimed the lives of 259 U.S. troops. Finally, the U.S. withdrew its forces from Lebanon by February 1984, and the French forces followed this withdrawal a few months later. Bombs, snipers, and bullets were still found across the Green Line between Muslims and Christians. Two years after Dodge's kidnapping, the succeeding President of the American University of Beirut, Malcolm Kerr, was shot dead on January 18, 1984, by what was claimed to be the al-Jihad al-Islami militia group along with the finding of a kidnapped member of the staff of the American University of Beirut two days later.

After a Military Council meeting in July 1984, the Druze and Amal militias began to withdraw their heavy weapons and artillery, and the Lebanese army took their place along the Green Line in West Beirut; this led to a complete withdrawal of the U.S. Marines by the end of July when they left Lebanon. It had been nine years since the bus attack in Ain Al Roumeneh, and shellings continued until this time. A columnist for the *An Nahar* newspaper described the mood in Lebanon in 1984 by writing, "There is nothing in the horizon except clouds and blood…Nobody has told us why the war has started or what the conditions for ending it are".

VIII. AUB President Malcolm H. Kerr, 1982-1984

Malcolm H. Kerr became AUB's President on July 1, 1982, after David Dodge was the Acting President for a year. In his first interim report Kerr wrote, "The period since the last Interim Report by the Acting President dated May 25, 1982, was dominated by the war in Lebanon and its consequences, including the kidnapping of Acting President David Dodge, the cancellation of summer school, the crisis in hospital operations and finances, and the rapid recovery of the University as the school year began".

The following month, Israel invaded Lebanon in June 1982, and as a result, the University canceled its final examinations, commencement exercises, and summer classes. Groups of armed men also occupied many parts of the AUB campus during Kerr's term; these armed men totaled a number of several hundred; these armed men were even controlling the traffic through the gates of the school. Kerr was advised to remain in the United States as he was pursuing his role as leader and President of AUB; he continued leading AUB from New York and Washington until he arrived in Beirut on August 28, 1982.

During the summer of 1982, many expatriate faculty members returned to their countries to escape the fighting, but their homes in Lebanon suffered damages. Also, the absent faculty members were not given their salaries or were given partial payment until the Government of Lebanon and the University administration processed it for them after pending decisions.

However, employees that remained on campus during such a period received a 6% raise in their salary.

During the Israeli invasion, the University did not allow the Israeli army men to enter the campus grounds. There was just one time that they were allowed to enter and that was to deliver emergency supplies of fuel at the request of the University. After the Israeli forces, Palestinians, and other unauthorized forces withdrew from Lebanon; the security situation on and off campus improved. The opening of classes was delayed for nine days until the University had the most significant number of faculty and students possible. A number of 4,509 students enrolled in Fall 1982 in comparison to 4,850 in the previous semester. The University also increased its student loan budget by 75% to assist students that could not afford an education at AUB.

In his first convocation address during the beginning of the semester on October 21, 1982, Malcolm Kerr made an inspiring speech to the AUB community. His speech was filled with optimism and he assured the AUB community that the campus and the streets outside of the school were safe, especially after the inauguration of a new Lebanese president that year. In his speech, Kerr stated, "No one threatens to turn the University into a military base, or to use violence against individual students and teachers. The atmosphere of fear and mistrust has evaporated…respect also the rights of this University as a place of thinking, not shouting, of learning, not speechmaking. The beauty of our campus lies in its cleanliness and dignity. Let it not be defaced with political slogans written on banners and walls that seek to impose simplistic dogma on others who do not share them…this is for the University's protection and for yours and that of your fellow students."

Soon after Kerr's inauguration, he held an all-day seminar to invite alumni and friends of the University and also traveled to Bahrain, Qatar, Abu Dhabi, and Dubai to address alumni and friends of the University about the conditions and problems that AUB was facing. He also discussed future systematic efforts by raising financial contributions for the University. Later on, the President traveled to the United States on December 28, 1982, and attended alumni gatherings in Los Angeles and San Francisco for the same cause. With the new President in office, Mr. Kerr sought various media coverage throughout his visits with senior government officials, universities, and other institutions. He also arranged many interviews with local and American journalists. AUB had always sought financial support from the United States, but Malcolm Kerr sought such support elsewhere. He called for assistance from Lebanon and the Arab world. According to Kerr, "These are the countries whose people we seek to serve. I believe in its high time for us to find ways of relying much more heavily

on our alumni and friends, and on business firms and governments

here in Lebanon and the Arab world, to support AUB, for AUB

belongs as much to them, or even more, than it does to anyone in

the United States".

Malcolm Kerr's major priorities focused on planning,

budgeting, administrative recruitment, development, and

government relations. The President continuously attended alumni

seminars in the United States as well as the Middle East in

countries such as Saudi Arabia, Kuwait, Bahrain, and Jordan.

President Kerr visited London with his assistant, Nazih Zeidan in

early July to meet with the Alumni Association, "The London

Friends of AUB" due to the slow developmental efforts that year.

As a result, two prominent alumni donated a total of $150,000 to

AUB. Also, a good number of panel discussions, lectures,

exhibitions, parties, and various student activities were held as a result of the decrease of strict security by the Lebanese Army and Internal Security Forces during this time. In October 1983, President Kerr formed the University Committee on Development that represented five faculty members and held several meetings to discuss ideas related to fund-raising and alumni activities.

To keep the students in the dorms equipped with proper entertainment and facilities, The President's Club Committee also met and provided the student dorms and clubs with a movie projector, a "Blind Students Room," and curtains and carpets for the West Hall building. The Information Office of AUB reported, "The activities of AUB President Malcolm Kerr were highlighted, including his interview, meetings and speeches on various occasions, as well as the role of AUB's Medical Center and its services to the community."

As Kerr had goals and plans to develop AUB, he was then shot twice at the back of his head by two unidentified gunmen while he was entering his office the morning of January 18, 1984.

IX. AUB a Major Target for Militiamen, 1985-1987

The ongoing kidnappings of Westerners were pursued during this time. On May 26, 1985, an English instructor at the American University of Beirut, Dennis Hill, 53 years old, was missing from his workplace and was later found on May 30, 1985, with six gunshot wounds in his head. Then, on June 9, 1985, another kidnapping took place, and the targeted American citizen was the AUB Dean of Agriculture, Thomas Sutherland. After this kidnapping, many other American faculty members fled the war-torn country. On July 1985, Syrian officers took part in assisting the Lebanese Government to collect arms from militias and also to close the offices that belonged to militias. Even the American

University of Beirut had military task forces sweeping through it to cleanse the University and the University's hospital. Also, by August 1985, more than 50 cases of abductions were reported to the police while others remained unreported. In the same month, shelling hit the lower sea-side campus of AUB and killed two students; it was uncommon for the University to be hit with shelling.

The body of the librarian, Peter Kilburn, who was kidnapped from AUB several months before, was found in April 1986; his body was bullet-ridden. The American University of Beirut was becoming a primary target for militias and gunmen. As a bus from the University's hospital was transporting staff and students from the hospital, gunmen ambushed the bus as it was headed towards the American University Hospital. "The gunmen entered the bus, carrying 40 doctors, nurses and other hospital and university staff members, and sprayed them with bullets from automatic weapons fitted with silencers, the police said. The killers escaped in a car." Four Lebanese citizens were dead as a result of this ambush in July 1986.

After classes were canceled due to the intensity of the war and kidnappings, Syrian troops came to the American University of Beirut to restore order. Syrian soldiers had taken control of all West Beirut, and during the next couple of days, they closed down 75 militia offices. Syrian commanders assured members of AUB's administration that they would secure the University.

These Syrian troops raided student dorms in search of hidden weapons which students would carry around with them on campus. Weapons were found, and some students were detained; these students belonged to many different militant factions. The University's faculty members were also threatened by students to raise their course grades. Faculty members were told by their students that if they did not respond to the student's request, then they would not make it home safely. Due to the presence of the Syrian security forces, the level of violence in West Beirut was reduced, but occasional shootings and explosions still occurred, some against Syrians.

X. AUB President Calvin H. Plimpton, 1984 – 1987

During the first year in which 65-year-old Calvin H. Plimpton led AUB, about thirty bombshells fell on the AUB campus. President Plimpton succeeded the former assassinated President, Malcolm Kerr. Plimpton, an American citizen, was a physician. A government figure, Mr. Nabih Berry, who was undergoing the investigation of the former assassinated President, was asked if more security would be provided for the new AUB President. Mr. Berry replied, "I honestly don't know, but security was improved on the campus after the assassination."

According to a 1984 article in the *Washington Post*, many faculty members grumbled at the thought of having Calvin Plimpton lead the University due to his old age; these faculty members were hoping to have someone younger and stronger to be able to handle the complications and chaos that the University was facing during this time of war.

In the first annual report, President Calvin began to change the custom of preparing annual reports taken from the three interim reports of the year, rather have it submitted at the end of every academic year with a summary of the year by the vice presidents, deans, and directors. President Calvin concluded in his 1984 annual report, "I am convinced that this procedure will provide the Trustees with an Annual Report which is far more meaningful and timely than the reports submitted during the last several years."

Although there were security issues, the President made sure that the University libraries were open for about 60 – 70 hours a week. Due to the events that took place that year, students attempted to bring their political controversies to the University grounds. Because of this, student life became abnormal. The leaders of the University, especially the Student Affairs Office tried to reason with these groups of students so that they maintain security and cooperation on campus. During President Plimpton's first academic year of leading the University, 1198 students were awarded degrees during graduation; however, no less than seven members of faculty and staff were abducted, and two members of AUB staff died because of the war.

A major achievement was the publication of over twenty books by faculty members that were given the opportunity to work together and produce these publications. President Plimpton took a different approach in his writings as he presented his Presidential reports. In his 1984-1985 yearly report, he wrote, "It would be unrealistic to avoid mention of the various tragedies and disasters enumerated above. However, it would be equally unrealistic and unprofitable to dwell on these negative developments. Therefore, the balance of this report will address itself to the positive developments at the University during the past year." This statement showed the optimism this President had. The accomplishments that were later mentioned by the President throughout the academic year of 1984 – 1985 included new requirements of introductory computer courses for all majors as well as computer literacy workshops for faculty and senior staff members. The President also offered to open this workshop for the public depending on the demand. Although the Faculty of Agriculture lost their Dean, Professor Thomas Sutherland, due to his abduction in which he was mistaken for President Plimpton, the President arranged for the students in this Department to return for a short session in AUB's Bekaa Valley farm, which was left

unattended by AUB's students and faculty due to the conflict.

Later, the students and faculty in the Agriculture Department spent

an entire semester on the farm to complete their practical work.

President Plimpton also made sure that the Office of Research and

External Programs was active and at the same time, this Office

administered contracts with governments and institutions outside

of Lebanon.

President Calvin Plimpton ended his report for the year

1984-1985 with a very positive and motivating note. He wrote,

"The report cannot come to an end without recognition of the

faculty, residents, interns, nurses, and staff in Faculty of Medicine

and in the Hospital, who have maintained a teaching and research

program while serving a tragically constant flow of casualties from

the strife in the country…each unit of the University has done

considerably more than merely survive. If a record such as that given in these pages can be complied in a year as was 1984-1985, then there is every reason to believe that we can work on towards the better future that inevitably lies ahead."

Public functions were held on campus, besides the adverse security conditions. Musicals, concerts, piano recitals, ballets, and public lectures were held during this academic year which brought normalcy on campus. According to the Office of Vice President for Administration, Plimpton's arrival to the University lifted morale and instilled a sense of direction and purpose. According to the Student Affairs Office, "Fighting in greater Beirut continued between conflicting groups, and this fighting resulted in still more tension among student groups on Campus, with consequent suspension of certain classes and several calls for a strike. Despite all of this, the University academic programs and University life were not seriously affected."

AUB's Office of Development reported that the President made many visits to countries such as Bahrain, Saudi Arabia, The United Arab Emirates, and Cyprus to reintroduce himself to the AUB Alumni and friends. President Plimpton also met with the royal families of the Gulf countries in support of AUB. Personal letters were sent to individual alumni members and gala dinners were also organized for the alumni outside of Lebanon. Alumni in the Gulf reacted favorably to the visits made, and it helped strengthen their attachment to AUB; their responses to AUB's appeal was encouraging, and checks continued to reach AUB in spite of the difficulties in the Lebanese postal system.

As a result of the killings and wounding of students on campus, President Plimpton sent a message stating that a university is a fragile institution which cannot withstand a succession of such tragedies. This message brought forth steadfastness in facing difficulties and challenges among the AUB community. Therefore, the University remained open as faculty, students, staff, and workers attended to their duties by fulfilling their mission the best way possible. Between the years of 1984 – 1985, the AUB Hospital admitted the largest number of casualties since the war started and remained to maintain a remarkable role.

In the 1985 – 1986 President Plimpton wrote in the opening lines of his report, "In my introduction to the Annual Report for 1984 – 1985, I noted that the academic year was a 'year of remarkable and tragic contrasts and contradictions.' One might have hoped for a lesser degree of such contrasts in 1985 – 1986, but, if anything, the year has proven to be a year of even greater extremes between the good and the bad." The President later mentioned that he was keen on remaining positive in his reports and intended to maintain positive developments more than the negative in his reports. Despite the tragic counts of more of AUB's community being attacked, killed, and abducted, the University had 5,033 students that attended classes in the first semester, and this figure rose the second semester with a total number of 5,235 students. As a result of these figures, the President stated in 1986, "There can be no better evidence of support for the University in the greater community than these figures; students and parents desperately need the continuity of the American University of Beirut."

President Plimpton was escorted out of Beirut with bodyguards and traveled to New York after several abductions of foreigners and university personnel. Plimpton always had armed bodyguards with him when he was in Lebanon, and he tried to keep his movements secret. While Plimpton was in the United States, he expected to fly back to Beirut and said, "My intention is to return to Beirut. The question is when." As the President was away from the warzone, he still remained to lead and make improvements to the University. The President also made sure that

AUB's Physical Plant produced three new water wells to supply water of high quality and quantity for the University. especially during the summer time to avoid chronic water shortages which was experienced years before. The President concluded in his yearly report of 1985-1986, "…the University will go on, with its normal programs and on schedule. This we shall do, in the hope that the Annual Report of 1986-87 will not be, once again, such a catalogue of contrasts and contradictions."

Some issues that students faced dealt with faculty leaves and replacements, tuition increase, security on campus, grades and threats, academic freedom of faculty members, and student discipline. The student dormitories were fully occupied, and a high demand for student housing was raised. To some extent, the student dormitories began to be filled by unauthorized militiamen. Many room-to-room inspections were made by the Dean of Students and other assistants with the authorization of the

President to rid or chase out these unauthorized militiamen from the dorms. Many rumors about the University closing down and transferring elsewhere spread after many grave events and abductions of faculty members; however, the President along with the Chairman of the Board of Trustees and the Office of Information helped each other by refuting these rumors to stakeholders and the public.

Many underestimated the President due to his old age since he was in his late 60s at the time; he was genial, very ironic, self-deprecating, and was very much into the New England tradition of the University. He was also courageous and defied the threat of kidnapping and assassinations and was still persistent in directing the University. What upset Plimpton was not the threat to his own safety, but the worrisome decline in academic standards at AUB. Students who were refused admission began threatening members of the admissions committee and students who were unhappy about their grades tried to intimidate their professors. In response to this circumstance, Calvin Plimpton said, "Our people are nervous. They are human. They don't want to risk themselves or their families. The question is how the dickens we can keep this place going?"

In the 1986 – 1987 Report of the President, President Plimpton remained in high spirits. He named every leader in charge of different sectors individually in his report and praised them for the different tasks they accomplished during that year. He also optimistically added, "The Syrian occupation of West Beirut has been important…there has been quiet in this portion of the city and on the campus, and normal living activities have returned. There is relative safety in walking the streets, and stores and restaurants have reopened. This has given AUB a much-needed breathing space, allowing us to think about things that universities should be thinking about, such as curriculum

and faculty skills and campus life, etc..”

The political intimidation of faculty and administration

became minimal that year, and the President was able to focus

more on academic quality rather than the Lebanese economy and

budgets. The enrollment level became at its highest, which came

close to 5,500 students. Plimpton noted, “It is hard not to take

some solace from this overwhelming expression of interest in

AUB.” The President also called for maintaining faculty and

staff remuneration along with the inflation of the country to

stabilize the cost of living for these important members of the

University. For this step to be taken, the cost of tuition had to be

increased along with revenues from all sources. Plimpton added,

“But if these necessary measures serve to curtail the exodus of

faculty, they will be worth it. Senior faculty remains our most

precious commodity – without this component all our efforts to restore quality to our academic programs will go for naught. Be that all as it may, we look forward to the coming academic year with optimism and good cheer." One of the opportunities which might have allowed a higher increase of student registration was the fact that the Board of Deans approved an extension of the deadline of application for applicants that found it difficult to commute to the University and apply; this might have been a significant aspect which assisted the increase of enrollment in 1987. After many years of struggling to keep outsiders and unauthorized students from the dorms, the Student Affairs Office was finally able to maintain full control of student residents and their unauthorized guests. A new dorm, Mary Dodge Hall, was also opened to accommodate 20 more female students.

President Plimpton was keen on his contacts with political figures by requesting that they do not send bombs to AUB grounds. Such political figures were Yasir Arafat, the PLO leader, the Israelis, as well as other political figures in the

Middle East. Plimpton was given a promise by them although

the AUB community was still able to hear bullets and bombs

flying by outside of the campus. For AUB not to receive many

shellings as one would expect, Plimpton gave advice and said,

"Lots of people (in Lebanon) would like to take us over…our

job is to stay outside the factions – not above or beneath them,

but outside. The main thing is to stay out of politics." In 1987,

President Plimpton resigned from the position of AUB President

but remained on the Beirut Board of Trustees. He was succeeded

by Fredrick Herter.

XI. 1988 – 1990

"America, the criminal should know that it will not get

away with what it is doing, especially in relation to the fate of the

hostages in our custody," as quoted from a letter sent to a Lebanese newspaper by a militia group. The Dean of AUB along with journalist, Terry Anderson, was still in custody at the time.

On January 1, 1989, fighting broke out between two Islamic militias and in the following month, two Christian forces battled each other. In the month of July 1989, about 250,000 people fled Lebanon to live abroad because their homes were shattered, and they were unable to cope with the ongoing shelling in the country. By this time, Syria began to occupy 70 percent of Lebanese territory and the war ceased to be between Christians and Muslims, but the Lebanese against the Syrian occupation. Another major tragedy was the assassination of Lebanese President Rene Mouawad as he was passing through a parade in his motorcade during the Lebanese Independence Day holiday on November 1989; he was later replaced by President Elias Hrawi.

Words of the promise of peace began to spread in Lebanon as the fighting stopped and warlords were exiled from the country, but many Lebanese still did not believe that peace would come to this country after so many years of war and fighting. On August 2, 1990, Iraq marched into Kuwait, and a whole new chapter began in the Middle East.

XII. AUB President Fredric P. Herter, 1987 – 1990

President Fredric Herter was a professor of surgery at the Colombia University College of Physicians and Surgeons before he succeeded former President Calvin Plimpton in 1987. President Herter did not immediately take up his residence on campus at the Marquand House, until he was given permission by some Lebanese government individuals to live on campus due to high-security alerts. Herter said that he would operate from the AUB New York office and work on fund-raising and development during his time there. During the beginning of his term, President Herter spoke with cautious optimism about AUB and mentioned the positive aspects about the University with regards to the high enrollment that the University was experiencing and he said, "This says that despite the hell Lebanon is going through, one of the most important passions of the Lebanese is education," he said, "and they want the best for their children."

The American University Hospital, which opened its doors to war victims, was attacked by a hidden bomb in a box of chocolates in November 1987. Seven people were killed while 31 were wounded as the bomb went off at a crowded cashier's office while people were paying bills for their relatives. President Frederic Herter was near Denver, Colorado visiting relatives at the time of the bombing and released a statement in response to the attack by calling all citizens of Lebanon to condemn this attack and join hands in developing a consensus for peace. Herter added, "We deplore the senseless and unconscionable act of terrorism which struck the American University Hospital today, crippling the very institution which through its doctors and staff rendered such selfless care to all the casualties of the civil strife during the past decade. Such barbarism is beyond understanding."

Besides the fact that terrorism existed around AUB grounds, the quality of academic and non-academic life on campus improved. MCAT examinations, used throughout the world, for medical applicants were introduced for the first time in AUB, and the scores of AUB candidates were encouragingly competitive with other candidates, worldwide. Extracurricular activities made an encouraging resurgence along with the dormant yearbook reappearing. President Hertner noted, "Political or sectarian activism was virtually absent, and travel between East and West Beirut was uninterrupted. For the first time in almost five years, the Trustees had an opportunity to meet and talk with students in person."

Although President Herter was unable to visit AUB grounds, he spent the year traveling to Athens, Greece to attend a conference in December 1987 which was the fifth "Support AUB Conference" held. At the end of February and early March 1988, President Herter visited the Gulf region and met with heads of states, government officials, alumni, and friends in Gulf countries such as Bahrain, The United Arab Emirates, Qatar, and Kuwait. These visits were to further develop and financially improve the University through financial support given by sole individuals from these regions. The Gulf was known to be economically stable and a prosperous region due to its petrol and job opportunities for Arabs, especially Lebanese that have fled Lebanon due to the war. Therefore, this region was a significant target for AUB, financially. Saudi Arabia gave a one million dollar donation, and the Kuwaiti government also made a one million dollar donation in support of the AUB Hospital.

Since President P. Herter led AUB while he was abroad, his relations with Arab political figures weakened, and eighty-five shells fell on University property over seven months between the years 1987 and 1988. Unlike, former President Calvin Plimpton who spent some time in Lebanon and made contacts with political leaders to avoid hurting University property by shellings and received promises that it would not be profoundly affected by mortars, Herter struggled with keeping the Campus mortar-free. U.S. relations with Lebanon were also weakening as many Lebanese did not agree with the U.S.'s policies. According to Adnan Iskandar, Vice President for University Relations, "The shelling of AUB might be intended as a political message to the U.S. government by one or more groups on the East side who are dissatisfied with some aspects of U.S. policy in Lebanon. The presence of Syrian soldiers on campus and the positioning of guns very close to the campus, could naturally be the cause of retaliatory shelling. Here again, the Administration has not been able to resolve this problem despite extensive contacts with various politicians and groups." Since problems were arriving among Syrian forces on campus and the Syrian forces were getting involved with various problems related to AUB and this involved AUB dealing with Syrian military and intelligence officers which was quite difficult for the AUB leadership. Adnan Iskandar advised in his 1988-1989 report, "I believe that relationships with the Syrian Government could be significantly improved through the designation of a liaison officer with whom the AUB Administration could deal exclusively. Such a liaison officer should be appointed by the political authorities in Damascus and should have the necessary status and authority to deal decisively with any problem that might arise. AUB should also appoint a liaison officer who would be responsible for all contacts with the

Syrian Government. Such a mechanism would certainly help to reduce the present tension in AUB-Syrian relations."

Since AUB is located in West Beirut, a Muslim area, AUB was accused of being biased since it catered to a majority of Muslims. As a result of this, it opened its doors to off-campus classes in the East Beirut region. AUB suffered what history will probably describe as its most calamitous academic year. Underground shelters such as basements of department buildings were put into much use during this year, while medical students were allowed to use the Hospital for housing. This major upheaval started on March 14, 1989, and forced suspension of teaching in all faculties except Medicine. Hopes to resume classes in May, June, August, and September or 1989 were all frustrated by the continuing violence, and the campus was, more than any other time in the fifteen years of civil war, the target of intermittent, but severe shelling which caused extensive damage. Although there was a suspension of classes for some time, the number of

permanent loss of faculty and students was small, and duties

continued to be carried out by devoted University faculty and staff

that risked their lives to resume work on campus to keep the

University functioning during difficult times. In 1989, the Dean of

Student Affairs, Dr. Fawzi Hajj reported, "Many students

volunteered their services to help other students, directing them to

safer places and providing necessary information for obtaining

food and transportation. Contracts were made with Government

officials and other leaders to arrange transportation for several

hundred students, to reach their homes in Lebanon and outside the

country as well. The University was indeed fortunate that there

were no casualties among the students, despite the fact that the

campus was heavily shelled…It was a difficult year – but it is

gratifying to see that the University survived, and we pray for

better conditions in Lebanon and a continuing strong AUB."

As mentioned earlier, an off-campus program was given in the East Beirut area for those who were unable to commute to West Beirut. Other courses such as business and computer science were offered in another city in Jounieh towards North Lebanon. This opportunity to educate and also give jobs for faculty to teach rather than driving a long distance past the Green- Line to reach AUB grounds, assisted in keeping AUB alive. It was convenient for students who wanted to pursue their education during times of war, and it also helped faculty and staff that needed their jobs and income close to home and less life-risking for them to commute to work.

Faculty were given opportunities by AUB to attend various workshops and conferences abroad for teaching development, and this was approved and funded by the University to pursue its quality in education regardless of the circumstances. As President Herter was sitting in his New York office, he wrote in the closing line of his 1988 – 1989 report, "I cannot close this report without

voicing, once again, our hurrahs and thanks to those intrepid

individuals in Beirut who kept the University alive during this

most difficult of difficult years. Thanks to them, AUB has been

granted yet another reprieve, and we look forward to the

challenges of building for a hopefully better day ahead."

According to Adnan Iskandar, the Deputy President and other

senior officials released many interviews to assure and emphasize

the continued commitment of AUB to its educational and

humanitarian role in Lebanon and the region to correct misleading

stories that the University would close its doors during its time of

turmoil.

Encouraging signs began to appear as the war started to

end. Over 600 students from the Off-Campus Program began to

register and show up to AUB grounds. In response to this, Herter

wrote in the 1989-1990 Report, "There are those who legitimately feel, at this time, that they cannot come to West Beirut, and there are families of students in East Beirut in such economic distress that the additional burden of commutation to Ras Beirut, and housing expenses on the campus, may make it impossible for them to send their children. We must provide help for them. Absolute security cannot, of course, be guaranteed to any student, but as of this writing, the Green Line has ceased to exist and the long-awaited militia-free security plane for greater Beirut appears on the verge of implementation. Transit should be safe". Many donations and gifts to restore the University and offer scholarships to students were made during this time. One of the major contributions made by the Rafic Hariri Foundation was AUB scholarships for around 1,400 students, along with other gifts from Gulf countries and Alumni Chapters worldwide.

During the years 1989-1990, work was done to resolve some issues that the University faced. Extension contacts were pursued with government officials at all levels and other political

groups in regard to an amendment of a new municipal tax law to

exempt AUB from building tax and this was approved. Another

agreement was made with the Lebanese security forces assigned to

AUB and this agreement allowed the University to discontinue the

practice of giving free meals to the members of the security forces

which would have the university save millions of Lebanese pounds

a year. Also, the end of pressure on AUB by some political groups

to receive special treatment in admissions, appointments, and

promotions was made. These issues were common during the time

of war and were finally put to an end for the benefit of the

University to resume financial and educational stability. For the

first time in ten years the University was able to hold a united

1989-1990 commencement outdoors on the AUB Green Field.

XIII. AUB President, Peter FitzGerald Dorman (2008-2014)

and the Arab Spring

Peter Dorman, a PhD graduate from the University of

Chicago, was a professor of history and archaeology at the

American University of Beirut. He became the 15th AUB President

by succeeding President John Waterbury. During his inauguration

speech on May 4, 2009, Dorman began his speech by reflecting on

AUB's late President Malcolm Kerr and the years of turmoil and

crisis AUB experienced during the civil war in Lebanon. He

gratefully looked back by saying, "The last inaugural address was

delivered by the late President Malcolm Kerr, twenty-five years

ago, at a time when the University and its values were very much

under threat. Those who have seen AUB through the crisis years of

the Lebanese civil war, who resolutely kept the classrooms open,

who devotedly served the hospital at risk of their lives, who

unselfishly gave of their wealth to ensure that this institution would not die, must feel enormous pride in the University today. We owe you a great debt of thanks for preserving the values and ideals that were established 142 years ago".

President Dorman emphasized how AUB must be the beacon of higher education by lighting the way for leaders of Lebanon as well as leaders in the region. He also brought three priorities in focus: 1. Faculty being empowered by their own research and seeking new knowledge, 2. Having a dynamic and diverse student body, and 3. Cultivating a responsive campus community to enhance the dialogue among all stakeholders of the University. Leadership and professional mastery play a significant role when it comes to accomplishing these priorities; according to Dorman, "This is the perennial quandary of any great university".

In recent years, a great increase of universities and graduate programs surged in many Middle Eastern and Gulf countries, and President Dorman believed that this has been as a result of AUB's historic success by also making it the American model of education in the Middle East and the Gulf region. Dorman closed his 2009 inauguration speech by saying, "And, finally, although it has survived a debilitating civil war, Lebanon still suffers from the entanglements of the unresolved Palestinian question south of its border, as well as continuing internal tensions, as recent events remind us. The lingering effects of this volatility foster a perception that Beirut remains an unsafe city and continue to blunt our attempts to recruit numbers of students and faculty from overseas. You will all have seen that the *New York Times* named Beirut as the world's number one travel destination for 2009, a ranking that astonished everyone—except those of us who live here. We have reason to hope that the recent rapprochement of President Obama's administration may herald a new period of understanding and dialogue between the United States and the great nations of the Middle East".

The year 2010 opened its doors to the start of an Arab Spring. The Arab Spring affected Middle Eastern and North African countries beginning when a Tunisian vegetable seller, Mohammed Bouazizi, individually protesting by setting himself on fire on December 17, 2010 in response to municipal officials that had confiscated his wares. As a result of this, Tunisia, Egypt, and Libya's governments toppled. Yemen and Syria also faced growing armed insurrection, while Bahrain was torn by strife. President Dorman looked back at this and in his 2011 opening ceremony speech he suggested, "It is too soon to measure or even fully imagine the implications of this sea-change; for each individual country the outcome is unpredictable. There are only two certainties: First, there will be no going back to the old autocratic regimes that once provided a measure of stability on the global stage; for they also demanded too much in the suppression of individual freedoms. Second, there will be no quick conversion to the open democratic societies Arab populations are yearning for:

that transformation will demand time and enormous patience, and

doubtless any number of false starts. But, let us acknowledge that

the Arab world has crossed an historical threshold, certainly the

most significant moment since the Palestinian *nakba* of 1948—and

perhaps even the breakup of the Ottoman Empire after World War

I, when its vast domains 3 were carved up and dispensed at will by

the victorious Allied nations. Whatever systems of government

appear in the aftermath of the Arab revolts, they will not be

imposed by outside powers. On the contrary, solutions will have to

be crafted by the inhabitants of each country, according to their

own aspirations. And it remains to be seen whether democratic

systems identical to those in the western world will serve as viable

models in the Middle East".

By September 2012, AUB ranked 250 in the world and had

a population of around 8,000 students; AUB's faculty also reached a total of 700. President Dorman made sure that the campus gates were wide open to educate not only the Lebanese, but the world. Social media has taken its toll in the world and President Dorman believed that personal journeys in higher education builds within us the tools that assess the kind of information we perceive from social media, only it is upon the students of the future to judge it, accept it, or discard it. He also claimed that broad reading is essential, so that it connects us with great thinkers who are no longer alive, and it also connects us with the journeys of the present and the past.

In an interview with President Dorman on April 13, 2013, President Dorman looked back at AUB's history of leaders and mentioned, "The leader I truly admire is Dr. Kerr. He was the one who had the deepest cultural understanding of the University's context. He was deeply devoted to the University. His assassination was a tragedy not only to AUB, but also to the country".

Dorman's leadership style was key to the development of a University that was picking up its pieces from years of political turmoil. AUB had a whole string of relatively short-term presidents, however, President Dorman saw that his style of leadership was similar to that of Dr. H. Bliss. According to Dorman, when Bliss took over after his father, Bliss took different steps; he made the College in more of a humanistic context. Bliss focused on the development of character and the direction he took AUB towards was a bit what Dorman was experiencing in 2013; this direction included transitioning to the university context, having personal responsibility, growing character, experiencing personal development, and committing to the community.

President Dorman faced challenges during the time of the Arab Spring; he had to ensure that there was a measure in academic objectivity and have appropriate academic discourse, which involved politics and social change. It was crucial that political emotions did not bubble over. At the beginning of the Arab Spring, Dorman considered that it was still easier to handle, however, by 2013 the number of Syrian students enrolled at AUB increased dramatically due to Syria being so close to home; as a result, some students at AUB supported the Assad Regime, while others supported the Opposition. The greatest challenge for Dorman was striking balance in academic enquiry and not letting events bubble over. There were a few student demonstrations on campus linked to the Arab Spring, so for Dorman to prevent future demonstrations from occurring, he reached out and spoke to students. When demonstrations happened, outside groups became involved and the AUB leadership took measures to keep outsiders off campus. The leadership also spoke to student leaders of different groups, and this helped prevent major demonstrations from happening during Dorman's term.

Dorman believed that it was very important for AUB presidents to have the qualities and the willingness to listen to all parties involved; "they need to listen deeply to what people say. The people, especially in Lebanon, are grateful when I sit, talk, pay attention, and deeply listen to what they have to say". Dorman added that listening brings understanding and a better atmosphere to reach a consensus and find a common position. Having the willingness to listen to different issues leads to finding common grounds.

During the interview, Dorman advised that is was very important for institutions of higher education that were caught up in the Arab Spring to embrace liberal arts, encourage students to think creatively, and to help students think broader than their civil society. "The role of AUB in the context of the Arab Spring is to prepare students for changes. It is important to restructure organizations and at the same time reflect on cultural traditions and history. I am dubious about Western models being transplanted in these countries. It is important to get young people to think about challenges and understand their responsibilities and rights in an open society. They should also take an active role to speak clearly and compassionately".

As the interview came to a close, Dorman mentioned that leaders are tested by what happens to them and that leadership skills can be taught and practiced, but what is more important are the values in leadership and how to make it relevant to the institution that a leader is leading. AUB has had strong values for more than 100 years, and effective leaders are those with personal values aligned with the institutional values.

XIV. Reflection

Today, Lebanon is still experiencing political conflicts and seemingly endless war; the American University of Beirut continues to be affected by the ongoing political conflict. Since the university's campus is located in the center of Beirut, it is a place where students fight or protest. Conflict occurs between students, especially between students who come from different religious backgrounds or sectors. According to *The New York Times* reporter, Marvine Howe, "Today the university is demonstrating the same resilience and resolve evident throughout the civil war. The school never completely shut down then, even in the darkest period of 1989, when classes were suspended for seven months, except for the school of medicine. AUB alumni, who kept the school's flame burning, can be found in the foremost medical centers in the United States and in key positions in government, business and academia throughout the Arab world".

Even after the assassination of former Prime Minister Rafiq El Hariri in 2005, AUB went ahead with its expansion plans of building new buildings for the expansion of new departments on campus. Former President of AUB, John Waterbury, called 2005 a year of tragedy during the 2005 graduation commencement but, also, a year of hope during which he presented diplomas to 1,688 graduates. President Waterbury was the fourteenth president of AUB and was the first president to reside in Beirut since 1984.

According to John Waterbury, 50 percent of the students came from around the Arab world, and the faculty had a strong American component. In 2005, he said the student body doubled and stood at 7,000, with 600 full-time faculty members, but 80 percent of the students and 75 percent of the faculty were Lebanese. After the September 11, 2001 tragedy in New York, there was a great flow of applicants from the Arab world, since these Arabs were either not allowed visas to travel to the United

States or because they were hesitant of consequences traveling to the United States.

Many of AUB's alumni have also proven themselves to be leaders in their fields throughout their educational and professional lives. AUB's alumni are found in different specialized areas such as politics, science, economics, business, and many more. Politicians like Waleed Jumblatt, Adel Osseiran, Selim al-Hoss, Najib Mikati and former Prime Minister Fouad Seniora and an endless list of members are found in the Lebanese government today and in the past. Basil Fuleihan was another unforgettable AUB Alumni who died in the same car as Prime Minister, Rafiq El Hariri. He was the Minister of Economy and Trade. Many people who come from different nationalities and have studied at this particular University, made an impact in their own communities and country.

While many students of different nationalities study in AUB, it is further distinguished by its integration of the sexes, which many Arab universities do not have. Many would be surprised to see how diverse the campus is. Students dress conservatively Islamic or outrageously Western. According to reporter Richard Covington, "Today, Beirut is arguably the most modern and vibrant capital of the Arab world, with an unsinkable entrepreneurial spirit and a near-palpable fever for urban renewal". Although many Lebanese students come from very poor backgrounds, they always tend to see a light at the end of the tunnel due to the educational opportunity they receive from AUB, and this offers them a better future with a better income.

The leaders of Lebanon are currently doing what they can to develop Lebanon and avoid future crisis, however for the country to develop, the leaders of the universities need to play a significant role in developing the system of higher education regardless of the troubled past it experienced.

AUB shifted from an Arabic speaking school to a liberal American English-speaking institution encouraging freedom of speech and analytical discovery to fit hand-in-hand with its motto, 'That they may have life, and have it more abundantly'. This American institution for the Middle East gives Arab nationals the opportunity to have empowerment and a voice (whether in Arabic or English) over their own education.

Bibliography

Al Assa'd, Sadik (1985). *The Annual Report of the American University of Beirut July 1, 1984 – June 30, 1985..* The American University of Beirut: Acting Director of Development

American University of Beirut. (1975 Aug 20). *New York Times*, p.60.

Anderson, Betty. (Sept 2008). Sept 1970 and The Palestinian Issue: A case study of student politicization at the American University of Beirut. *Civil Wars, Vol.10 Issue 3*.

Andrews, John (1996). Outside influence. *Economist, 338*.

Al-Huzaim, Dr. Yusef bin 'Othman. (2011). The Principles of Leadership. Riyad, KSA: Darussalam

Altbach, Philip G., Berdahl, R. O., & Gumport, P. J. (2005).

American Higher Education in the Twenty-First Century: Social,

Political, and Economical Challenges

(2nd ed.). Baltimore, Maryland: The John Hopkins University

Press.

Beirut Fighting Grows; Battles Spread to Hotel Area, Outlying

Town Gunfire Engulfs Beirut. (1976 Jan 11). *The Washington Post*,

p. 1.

Becker, B., Dawson, P., Devine, K., Hannum, C., Hill, S., Leydens,

J., et al. (2005). *Case studies.*

Between Devil and Deep Blue Sea. (13 Dec 1975). *The Economist.*

P. 58.

Blakemore, William. (2 Jan 1976). American University wins vital

aid from Beirut. *The Christian Science Monitor*, p. 8.

Campbell, Colin. (21 June 1985). Hostages in Lebanon: an endangered campus; fears for American University rise: can it survive the Beirut violence? *The New York Times*, p.11

Claiborne, William. (16 Dec 1975). Beirut University Seeks Funds, Cease-Fire. *Washington Post*, p. A3.

Covington, Richard (April 2000). Beirut rises from the ashes. *Smithsonian, 31*.

Cowan, James W. (1976). *President's Report/Interim Board of Trustees: Interim Report of Period from March 16 to June 15, 1976.* The American University of Beirut: Acting President.

Deitch, Joseph. (2 Jul 1985). Academic freedom in embattled Beirut. Amid political chaos, American University in Beirut is 'island of sanity'. *Christian Science Monitor,* p. 3

Denton, Herbert H (1984 Apr 15). Where Beirut War Began, Christians See No End. *The Washington Post.* p. A1

Fiedler, F.E. (1992). Time-based measures of leadership experience and organizational performance: A review of research and a preliminary model. *Leadership Quarterly*, 3, 5-23.

Fisk, Robert B. (1975 Dec 3). *New York Times*, p. 41.

Fricke, Adrienne (May 2005). Forever Nearing the Finish Line: Heritage Policy and the Problem of Memory in Postwar Beirut. *International Journal of Culture Property, Vol.12.*

Khan IV, Aga (1976 Feb 21). What the War Cost. *The Economist.* p. 51

Gall, M., Gall, J., & Borg, W. (2003). *Educational research: An introduction.* (2003 ed., p. 595). Boston: A and B.

Ghosn, Raymond S. (1975). *President's Report/Interim Board of Trustees.* The American University of Beirut: Department of Engineering and Architecture.

Graham, Bradley. (1984). Hanging On in Beirut; Some Americans Stay In Face of Terrorism. *The Washington Post.* p. A1.

Haddadin, M.J. (1987). *The Annual Report of the American University of Beirut* 1986 -1987. The American University of Beirut: Vice President for Academic Affairs

Haddadin, M.J. (1989). *The Annual Report of the American University of Beirut* 1988 -1989. The American University of Beirut: Vice President for Academic Affairs

Hajj, Fawzi M. (1986). *The Annual Report of the American University of Beirut* 1985 – 1986. The American University of Beirut: Dean of Students

Hajj, Fawzi M. (1987). *The Annual Report of the American University of Beirut* 1986 – 1987. The American University of Beirut: Dean of Students

Hajj, Fawzi M. (1989). *The Annual Report of the American University of Beirut* 1988 – 1989. The American University of Beirut: Dean of Students

Hajj, Fawzi M. (1990). *The Annual Report of the American University of Beirut* 1989 – 1990. The American University of Beirut: Dean of Students

Hakim, George. (1975). *President's Report/Interim Board of Trustees*. The AmericanUniversity of Beirut: Vice President.

Hammer, Joshua (2008). Precarious. *Lebanon, Vol. 39*.

Herter, Frederic P. (1987). *Annual Report of the American University of Beirut 1987 – 1988.* The American University of Beirut: Report of the President

Herter, Frederic P. (1989). *Annual Report of the American University of Beirut 1988 –1989.* The American University of Beirut: Report of the President

Herter, Frederic P. (1990). *Annual Report of the American University of Beirut 1989 –1990.* The American University of Beirut: Report of the President

Hijazi, Ihsan A. (1976 Jan 25). Banks Also a Casualty in Lebanon. *The New York Times*, p. 167.

Hijazi, Ihsan A. (1985 May 30). Gemayal Has Narrow Escape as His Palace is Bombarded. *The New York Times*, p. 1.

Hijazi, Ihsan A. (1985 June 11). The 8th American is Kidnapped by Beirut Gunmen.*The New York Times*, p.1

Hijazi, Ihsan A. (1986 July 20). 4 Killed in Attack on Bus in Beirut. *The New York Times*, p. 3.

Hijazi, Ihsan A. (1987 Mar 15). Syrians revive Sense of Order at Campus in Beirut. *The New York Times,* p.16.

Hijazi, Ihsan A. (1989 Jul 31). Amid an 'Inferno of Bombs,' With Nowhere Safe, 250,000 Flee Beirut in a Week. *The New York Times*, p.7.

Hirst, David. (2010). *Beware of Small States: Lebanon, Battleground of the Middle East.* England: Faber and Faber.

Hoff, Kathryn S. (1999). Leaders and managers: essential skills required within higher education. *Higher Education,* p. 319.

Howe, M. (December 2005). The American University of Beirut: A Year of Tragedy and Hope. *Washington Report on Middle East Affairs, 24*.

Howe, Marvin. (19 April 1987). New head is named for Beirut school. *The New York Times,* p. 1.

Ignatius, David. (28 Sept 1986). Kidnapping a University in Beirut; When Islamic Jihad Grabs AUB Officials, It Is Attacking Us All. The Washington Post, C2.

Iskandar, Adnan. (1989). *Annual Report of the American University of Beirut 1988 –1989.* The American University of Beirut: Vice President for University Relations

Iskandar, Adnan. (1990). *Annual Report of the American University of Beirut 1989 –1990.* The American University of Beirut: Vice President for University Relations

Kamguian, A. (2001). *Religion in education—A case study*. Based

on a speech given at a seminar held by Save the Children in

Stockholm on October 5, 2001.

Kennedy, Michael J (1983 February 16). Lebanon Army Begins

Patrolling East Beirut; Takes Full Control of Capital Since '75-76

Civil War. *Los Angeles Times*, p. B1.

Kidnapings Spur Beirut Battle. (1975 Dec 25). *The Washington

Post*, A14.

Kooley, John K. (1975 Nov 25). Conflict Hurts American

University of Beirut. *Christian Science Monitor*, p.3

Lamb, David (1983 September 2). Lebanese Soldiers Retake West

Beirut From Muslims. *Los Angeles Times*, p. A10.

Main Gate: American University of Beirut Magazine. (Winter

2008). p.64.

Malik, Habib C. (1989 Aug 20). The Real Conflict in Lebanon's War; It's Not Moslem Against Christian -- It's Both Against Syrian Domination. *The Washington Post*, P.B1.

Mawlawi, Radwan. (1986). *The Annual Report of the American University of Beirut* 1985 – 1986. The American University of Beirut: Office of Information Director

Meyer, Raymond S. (1976). *President's Report/Interim Board of Trustees*. The American University of Beirut: Director of Operations.

Merriam, S. B. (1998). *Qualitative research and case study applications in education* (Rev. ed.). San Francisco: Jossey-Bass.

Mintzberg, H. (1983). *Power in and around organizations*. Englewood Cliffs, NJ: Prentice Hall.

Mishalani, Richard. (1976). *President's Report/Interim Board of Trustees*. The American University of Beirut: The Physical Plant.

Morris Jr., Joe A. (1976 Jan 11). Lebanon Civil War Regaining Past Fury. *Los Angeles Times (1886-Current File)*, p.5.

Musa, Hind. (1976). *President's Report/Interim Board of Trustees*. The American University of Beirut: Report from Student Affairs.

O'Ballance, Edgar. (1998). *Civil War in Lebanon, 1975-92*. New York, New York: Palgrave Macmillan.

Pace, Eric. (1984). American University of Beirut Replaces its Slain President. *New York Times*. p. 4.

Plimpton, Calvin. (1984). *The President's Annual Report to the Board of Trustees 1983 – 1984*. The American University of Beirut.

Plimpton, Calvin. (1985). *Annual Report of the American University of Beirut 1984 –1985.* The American University of Beirut.

Plimpton, Calvin. (1986). *Annual Report of the American University of Beirut 1985 – 1986.* The American University of Beirut.

Plimpton, Calvin. (1987). *Annual Report of the American University of Beirut 1986 – 1987.* The American University of Beirut.

Registrar's Periodic Report (May 1976). *President's Report/ Interim Board of Trustees.* The American University of Beirut.

Rodenbeck, Judith F (2007). In This Issue: Crossing Memory's Green-Line-Contemporary Art in Beirut. *Art Journal, Vol. 66.*

Salem, Elie A. (18 May 1976). *The President's Report/Interim Board of Trustees.* The American University of Beirut: Faculty of Arts and Sciences.

Sale, J. E.M., Lohfeld, L. H., & Brazil, K. (2002). Revisiting the quantitative-qualitative debate: Implications for mixed-methods research. *Quality & Quantity, 36,* 43-53.

Salti, Ibrahim S.(1989). *Annual Report of the American University of Beirut 1988 –1989.* The American University of Beirut: Deputy President

Salti, Ibrahim S.(1990). *Annual Report of the American University of Beirut 1989 –1990.* The American University of Beirut: Deputy President

Stake, R.E. (2000). Case studies. In N.K. Denzin & Y.S. Lincoln (Eds.), *Handbook of Qualitative research* (2nd ed., pp.435-454). Thousand Oaks, CA: Sage.

Tanner, Henry (1976 May 28). Sister of Moslem Leader is Murdered in Lebanon; Leader's Sister is Slain in Beirut. *New York Times*, p. 41.

Tanner, Henry (1976 June 9). Decency and Courage Amid Lebanese Horror: Much Courage Amid Horror in Lebanon. *New York Times*, p. 1.

The Pressure Builds on Lebanon, The Marines and the President. (1984 Feb 5). *New York Times*, p. E1

The Board of Academic Deans. (2 June 1976). *The President's Report/Interim Board of Trustees*. The American University of Beirut.

The New York Times. (31 Dec 1975). P. 4.

The New York Times. (18 Feb 1976). P. 9.

The New York Times. (26 July 1985). P. 6.

The New York Times. (15 Nov 1987). P. 3.

The New York Times. (22 Oct 1988). P. 1.

The New York Times. (15 Nov 1987). P. 3.

The San Diego Tribune. (13 Aug 1985). P. A-10.

The San Diego Tribune. (25 Apr 1986). P. A-4.

Weber, M. (1947). *The theory of social and economic organizations*. Translated by T. Parsons. New York: Free Press.

Whitman, Arthur H. (1 June 1976). *Newsletter 1975 – 1975 No. 4: President's Report/Interim Board of Trustees*. The American University of Beirut: AUB Trustees.

Winslow, Charles (1996). *Lebanon: War and Politics in a Fragmented Society*. New York, New York: Routledge.

Wolcott, H.E. (2001). *Writing up qualitative research* (2nd ed.). Thousand Oaks, CA:Sage.

Yukl, Gary. (2006). *Leadership in Organizations*. 6th ed, University of Albany, State State University of New York: Pearson Education International.

Zachs, F. (2005 August). From the Mission to the Missionary: The Bliss Family and the Syrian Protestant College (1866-1920). *Welt des Islams, 45*.

Zeidan, Nazih (1988). *Annual Report of the American University of Beirut 1987-1988*.

The American University of Beirut: Director of Development

Zeidan, Nazih (1989). *Annual Report of the American University of Beirut 1988-1989*.

The American University of Beirut: Director of Development

Zigarmi, Drea, O'Connor, M, Blanchard, K. & Edeburn, C. (2005).

The Leader Within:Learning enough about yourself to lead others.

Upper Saddle River, New Jersey: Pearson Prentice Hall.

600,000 Lebanese Fled Abroad. (1977 April 23). *New York Times,*

p. 5.

(2005 May 25). History. The American University of Beirut Web

site.

www.ingramcontent.com/pod-product-compliance
Lightning Source LLC
Chambersburg PA
CBHW031230250726

48655CB00005B/1887